The FC&S

Q&A

Book

Never Before Published
Property & Casualty Questions

Real Q&A's
for Real People

From The Editors of
FC&S

Diana Reitz • David Thamann • Susan Massmann • Christine Barlow

Copyright © 2007 by
THE NATIONAL UNDERWRITER COMPANY
P.O. Box 14367
Cincinnati, Ohio 45250-0367

International Standard Book Number: 978-0-87218-736-8
Library of Congress Control Number: 2007926639

Printed in the United States of America

TABLE OF CONTENTS

PERSONAL LINES

HOMEOWNERS

PERSONAL AUTO

COMMERCIAL LINES

COMMERCIAL GENERAL LIABILITY

BUSINESS AUTO

GARAGE

COMMERCIAL PROPERTY

MISCELLANEOUS

CRIME

WORKERS COMPENSATION

Personal Lines

HOMEOWNERS

Insured Moved, Leaving Relative in House; Is There Coverage?

Homeowner has moved to her fiancé's house w/2 children. Her own house remains occupied by her 20 yr. old daughter while it is for sale. Is there coverage for the dwelling, contents and loss of use (e.g. an apartment for the daughter)?

Is there an obligation for the named insured to notify the insurer of her move during the policy period or is it appropriate to notify upon policy renewal?

North Carolina Subscriber

While most insurers would rather have a "for-sale" dwelling occupied than not, there are some coverage issues here should a loss occur.

First, the home is no longer owner-occupied. The daughter is no longer an "insured," since she's no longer a member of her mother's household. So, while the mother's personal property would be covered in the dwelling (coverage C applies anywhere in the world), except for theft coverage, the daughter's would not.

I believe in this situation I'd contact the underwriter to see if he or she could note the file to extend coverage for the dwelling and the daughter's property for a time (when I was an underwriter we would allow three months, and then perhaps for a good client a little longer; after that we would require a dwelling fire policy). If agreeable, then perhaps after an agreed-upon time re-write the dwelling on a fire policy, with a tenant homeowners for the daughter.

Dead Body vs. Pollutants

Is there any exclusion under the standard HO 3 policy that would apply to the following: one of the two named insureds on a policy commits suicide, requiring that biohazard clean up is done.

Oklahoma Subscriber

In the definition given for "pollutants," all of the things mentioned: "solid, liquid, gaseous or thermal irritant or contaminant, including smoke, vapor, soot, fumes, acids, alkalis, chemicals and waste. Waste includes materials to be recycled, reconditioned or reclaimed..." are those commonly associated with environmental pollution caused by a manufacturing process.

3

The pollutants are man-made (as opposed to caused by a deceased body).

So, no exclusion applies to cleanup of the dwelling.

But with regard to the contents, a named peril must be the cause of loss. If the suicide was caused by gunshot, then the named peril of "explosion" would be the cause; if not, then no coverage.

Cleanup Coverage for Dead Body— Dwelling and Property

We have an insured under an HO 03 04 91 policy form. This insured, a 270 pound man dropped dead in the house and was not discovered for about 10 days. The loss occurred in the San Bernardino area of California, a desert like area. The body was badly decomposed when it was discovered and many of the deceased's bodily fluids had leaked out and the emergency personnel tracked the fluids around while getting the body out.

The HO 03 04 91 is an all risk type of policy. The claims handler thinks that there may be an exclusion for this type of damage under the Perils Insured Against exception section 2. E. 5), copied here for you convenience. (5) Discharge, dispersal, seepage, migration, release or escape of pollutants unless the discharge, dispersal, seepage, migration, release or escape is itself caused by a Peril Insured Against under Coverage C of this policy.

SECTION I - PERILS INSURED AGAINST COVERAGE A - DWELLING and COVERAGE B - OTHER STRUCTURES

We insure against risk of direct loss to property described in Coverages A and B only if that loss is a physical loss to property. We do not insure, however, for loss:

e. Any of the following:

Pollutants means any solid, liquid, gaseous or thermal irritant or contaminant, including smoke, vapor, soot, fumes, acids, alkalis, chemicals and waste. Waste includes materials to be recycled, reconditioned or reclaimed; (6) Settling, shrinking, bulging or expansion, including resultant cracking, of pavements, patios, foundations, walls, floors, roofs.

The contents are named peril as follows:

COVERAGE C - PERSONAL PROPERTY

We insure for direct physical loss to the property described in Coverage C caused by a peril listed below unless the loss is excluded in SECTION I - EXCLUSIONS.

1. *Fire or lightning.*

2. *Windstorm or hail.*

   This peril does not include loss to the property contained in a building caused by rain, snow, sleet, sand or dust unless the direct force of wind or hail damages the building causing an opening in a roof or wall and the rain, snow, sleet, sand or dust enters through this opening. This peril includes loss to watercraft and their trailers, furnishings, equipment, and outboard engines or motors, only while inside a fully enclosed building.

3. *Explosion.*

4. *Riot or civil commotion.*

5. *Aircraft, including self-propelled missiles and spacecraft.*

6. *Vehicles.*

7. *Smoke, meaning sudden and accidental damage from smoke.*

   This peril does not include loss caused by smoke from agricultural smudging or industrial operations.

8. *Vandalism or malicious mischief.*

9. *Theft, including attempted theft and loss of property from a known place when it is likely that the property has been stolen.*

   This peril does not include loss caused by theft:

   a. *Committed by an "insured";*

   b. *In or to a dwelling under construction, or of materials and supplies for use in the construction until the dwelling is finished and occupied; or*

   c. *From that part of a "residence premises" rented by an "insured" to other than an "insured."*

This peril does not include loss caused by theft that occurs off the "residence premises" of:

a. Property while at any other residence owned by, rented to, or occupied by an "insured," except while an "insured" is temporarily living there. Property of a student who is an "insured" is covered while at a residence away from home if the student has been there at any time during the 45 days immediately before the loss;

b. Watercraft, and their furnishings, equipment (45 days to give notice) and outboard engines or motors; or

c. Trailers and campers.

10. Falling objects.

This peril does not include loss to property contained in a building unless the roof or an outside wall of the building is first damaged by a falling object.

Damage to the falling object itself is not included.

11. Weight of ice, snow or sleet which causes damage to property contained in a building.

12. Accidental discharge or overflow of water or steam from within a plumbing, heating, air conditioning or automatic fire protective sprinkler system or from within a household appliance.

This peril does not include loss:

a. To the system or appliance from which the water or steam escaped;

b. Caused by or resulting from freezing except as provided in the peril of freezing below; or

c. On the "residence premises" caused by accidental discharge or overflow which occurs off the "residence premises."

In this peril, a plumbing system does not include a sump, sump pump or related equipment.

13. Sudden and accidental tearing apart, cracking, burning or bulging of a steam or hot water heating system, an air conditioning or automatic fire protective sprinkler system, or an appliance for heating water.

We do not cover loss caused by or resulting from freezing under this peril.

14. *Freezing of a plumbing, heating, air conditioning or automatic fire protective sprinkler system or of a household appliance.*

    This peril does not include loss on the "residence premises" while the dwelling is unoccupied, unless you have used reasonable care to:

    a. *Maintain heat in the building; or*

    b. *Shut off the water supply and drain the system and appliances of water.*

15. *Sudden and accidental damage from artificially generated electrical current.*

    This peril does not include loss to a tube, transistor or similar electronic component.

16. *Volcanic eruption other than loss caused by earthquake, land shock waves or tremors.*

?
I don't see where there will be coverage for the personal property, but I do think that there will be coverage for the Structure, as it is not specifically excluded. Do you agree?

California Subscriber

The loss to the dwelling (but not to any personal property) is covered. If you look at the policy definition for pollutants, it states these are "solid, liquid, gaseous or thermal irritant or contaminant, including smoke, vapor, soot, fumes, acids, alkalis, chemicals and waste. Waste includes materials to be recycled reconditioned or reclaimed." Note that these are all by-products of a manufacturing process, not of natural decomposition of a body. So, there is coverage to clean up the floor or walls, but since contents are covered on a named peril basis and no named peril applies, there is no coverage for any cleanup of contents.

Tree Roots and Collapsed PVC Line

?
The policy holder incurred a loss to the outgoing water waste line as tree roots eventually collapsed the PVC line. As a result, the water backed up and the policy holder must now replace the collapsed line as well as deal with the water damage loss. The carrier has acknowledged coverage for the water damage. The carrier notes that tree roots infiltrating a sewer line and the cost to maintain that sewer line are normal maintenance costs associated with owning and maintaining a home. They further note this type of normal wear & tear to a sewer line is not a fortuitous loss.

The homeowners' contention seems to be a rational one. First, the PVC pipe did not deteriorate. The loss was in fact fortuitous because the collapse was sudden and accidental. How was the insured to maintain an underground PVC pipe?

The bulk of the insured's claim is the expense associated with the excavation of the ground to repair and replace the damaged line. The carrier will not pay for this.

We would like your opinion regarding their position.

Wear, tear, marring and deterioration are not covered relative to this exclusion; the policy goes on to state:

If any of these cause water damage not otherwise excluded, from a plumbing, heating, air conditioning or automatic fire protective sprinkler system or household appliance, we cover loss caused by the water including the cost of tearing out and replacing any part of the building necessary to repair the system or appliance.

We do not cover loss to the system or appliance from which the water escaped.

Would the excavation costs be covered?

Kentucky Subscriber

The insurer is correct. It is a given that tree roots will grow toward a water source, so the loss is not fortuitous. In other words, the loss will occur; it is just a question of when. Thus, it is not like, say, a fire or windstorm which might or might not cause a loss.

So, the "wear and tear" exclusion, and also the exclusion for faulty or improper maintenance apply. But, as the insurer has noted, any loss not otherwise excluded is covered, so the water damage from the water which was unable to be transported off the premises is covered.

However, it is possible to find coverage for the costs to excavate the pipe (but not the actual replacement) under the additional coverage for reasonable repairs. This coverage says that if covered property is damaged by a peril insured against, which it was, then the insurer will pay "reasonable cost incurred by [the named insured] for necessary measures taken solely to protect against further damage."

Tree Roots and Sewer Line

We have several claims recently that are under a DP-3 (07/88) policy form. The claim arises from the insured's tree roots damaging the insured's sewer line or the sewer line breaking and the roots entering. Neither the DP-3 nor any of the endorsements speak directly to this situation. There is the wear and tear language in the policy and that may apply. Is there any case law, the losses are in California that may apply to the loss?

California Subscriber

The problem with tree roots is that they will grow toward a source of water. It's not a case of "might grow"; they *will* grow. Thus, a loss caused by them is not fortuitous and is not insurable. The closest exclusion is "wear and tear," but "faulty maintenance" also applies. However, with each of these exclusions, any ensuing loss not otherwise excluded is covered. So, if there was resulting water damage, that damage could be covered.

The only case law I found had to do with whose responsibility it was to eliminate tree roots growing from one landowner's land to another's, or, when a municipality planted a tree on top of a sewer line, whose responsibility it was to repair the homeowners' damaged sewers (the municipality's--it should have known better).

Tree Limbs Over Roof

The insured's neighbor's tree limbs hang over on the insured's roof. Over time, the limbs and leaves caused one area of the roof shingles to deteriorate to the point that felt is visible. No other area of the roof has any other damage. The HO-3 policy excludes 'wear and tear' and 'weather conditions' (limited exclusions) but there is no exclusion found specifically for this damage caused by trees. The resulting roof damage is obviously from numerous 'events' and no one single event. However, the policy defines 'occurrence' as 'an accident, including continuous or repeated exposure to substantially the same general harmful conditions, which results, during the policy period, in:

b. "Property damage".

Based on the above, (a) would the loss be covered? and (b) would one deductible apply or would numerous deductibles apply?

Indiana Subscriber

9

First, the standard homeowner's forms define "occurrence," but you will note that this word in quotations appears only in section II liability coverage. It does not appear in the section I property coverages.

I believe this loss is not covered. The exclusion for "wear and tear" would not appear to apply in and of itself, since the loss is clearly in one section of the roof.

But there are two other places to look. The first is the exclusion for faulty or inadequate maintenance, which led to the "wear and tear" (excluded) of the section of roof. The other is the exclusion for "neglect." It would appear that the insured could easily have noticed there was a problem, and cleared away the limbs, leaves, or even cut down the offending tree branches.

Most courts are of the opinion that the property owner has the right to do whatever he will with branches (or fruit) overhanging his property.

The insured might wish to turn to his neighbor's homeowners policy. The additional coverage for property damage (essentially no-fault good neighbor coverage) could apply, as could the neighbor's liability provided the insured told the neighbor the tree was damaging his roof.

Water—Broken Water Main-Home and Farm

A water main located on neighboring property servicing neighboring property (not the insured in any manner), ruptured underground. The water traveled to the surface onto the insureds property and caused building damage. The issue at hand is what peril to apply to the loss. Enclosed is a section of the policy dealing with the Named perils for Coverage. The policy is split into two sections. One covering the Home and one covering the Farming Buildings. The named Perils covering the home range from A-S but on the Farm Buildings A-R.

The two perils in question are Peril C and Peril P-5. The argument for Peril C is that it is undefined within the policy. Several sources (Webster, Wikipedia) give definitions that would be applicable to what a 6" main line water feed pipe would experience in order for it to split. The descriptions from the repair company of the feed pipe support explosion versus a cracking, splitting, or rotted pipe.

I believe there is sufficient evidence to confirm that the pipe suffered an increase in pressure which caused it to break apart.

The issue is if the Peril for Explosion is in case history anywhere, either way? The other would be if you would agree with the stance that the Proximate

Cause of the loss (assuming all facts supporting the break) is the Explosion and that that resulting event is the discharge of water. If so, would you opinion that coverage exits for the water damages to the insured property?

Ohio Subscriber

With regard to the farm buildings, it is possible that the cause of loss could be considered "explosion." *Webster's Collegiate* defines "explosion" as "an exploding; esp. a blowing up or bursting with a loud noise." Note that there is no mention of gunpowder or fire, for example. However, with named perils, it is up to the insured to prove that explosion was indeed the proximate cause of the water damage, and, because there is a possible applicable cause of loss off-setting the exclusion for accidental discharge occurring off-premises, the ambiguity leads to coverage.

It is much easier with the coverage for damage done to the home itself; the coverage here is on an "open perils" basis and no exclusion applies.

Water – Plumbing Leak Inside Wall/Old Pipes

The insured turns in a plumbing leak claim within a bathroom. The leak originates inside the wall cavity and is not noticed until water shows up on the adjoining Kitchen floor. The pipes are 60+ years old. Some of the damages are consistent with a repeated seepage over a long period of time and others are the type which occurs from a sudden and accidental pipe leak. The question is due you deny the damages (rotten wood) that can easily be determined to be caused from the long term leak but then give the insured the benefit of the doubt and pay for damages that were or could have been caused from a one time occurrence? So complete denial or a partial denial?

Pennsylvania Subscriber

Nationwide does not totally follow ISO's wording, so you will have to check how the homeowners form in question reads. For example, under the ISO 2000 homeowners, the loss, including the wet rot, would be covered since it is the result of a plumbing leak and hidden within the walls. If the endorsement for limited fungi and wet rot is attached, there is still coverage provided the damage was hidden.

But if your form states that there is no coverage for damage from repeated seepage or leakage over a period of weeks, months, or years, then I agree that the obviously long-term damage would not be covered, but the damage that could have been caused from a one-time occurrence would be covered.

This seems the fairest settlement for your insured.

Broken Pipe and DP 3, Tenants Moved

The policy form is a 7/88 DP3, residence is tenant occupied. Tenant moved out in August; property was fine in August and September; October 25, water was found gushing from a broken hose damaging carpeting, flooring etc. Property was vacant more than 30 days. Is this constant or repeated seepage or leakage over a period of weeks/months and excluded?

Oklahoma Subscriber

Seepage is defined as the process of seeping, which is to pass slowly through fine pores or small openings. The definition of leakage is to enter or escape through an opening usually by a fault or mistake; while this is broader, the intent of the policy is to exclude slow and regular flow of water over an extended period of time. In your description of the loss as a hose breaking, that is sudden and accidental and not seeping or leaking, so there would be coverage. Even if the hose broke due to wear and tear, the repair of the hose would not be covered but the resultant water damage to the rest of the dwelling would be.

Pipes Leaking Under Slab of Home on DP 2

Pipe(s) under house that was built on a slab are leaking. No water damage as of yet. Insured noticed that her water bill was high and plumber tested the lines. This is on a DP-2, named peril policy. While sudden and accidental discharge of water is a covered peril, this is likely a long-term leak; however, under the peril of accidental discharge, the policy states that we cover to tear out whatever part of the structure necessary to replace the pipes. Does the peril of accidental discharge have to have occurred in order to trigger the tear out coverage? And, if the insured is going to replace all lines under the house, rather than try to fix the one that is leaking (being done to avoid going into the slab), does the cost to cut into the house to run new lines fall under the coverage afforded under that peril?

Kentucky Subscriber

You do not state which DP form is in effect, so I'm answering two ways.

First, if the DP 00 02 12 02 is in force, then there is no coverage for the loss as you describe it. Yes, "accidental discharge" is a named peril, but it must cause physical damage to the covered property. You say that there is no water damage, so this becomes a maintenance problem for the insured.

But if the form is the DP 00 02 07 88, an argument can be made for coverage--the accidental discharge is causing the insured to lose personal property, the water for which he has paid, and thus there is coverage for the tear-out. If the insured elects to run new lines, I do not think you owe for that cost. In that case, you would pay the amount you would have owed had the insured done the tear-out, but the additional cost would be borne by the insured.

Broken Pipe under Slab and HO 00 08

I know HO8 doesn't cover water damage, but if there's a broken drain pipe under the slab, is that covered?

Montana Subscriber

The HO 00 08 might respond to covering the broken drain pipe under the slab, but the insured would have to prove that one of the named perils was responsible for causing the break. For example, if by some stretch the pipe was damaged by fire, that would be covered, but if it broke simply because of "wear and tear" that would not be.

Lightning Strike to Pipes

I have an insured with an HO3 (4-91) who is claiming a lightning strike caused damage to the piping from the well to the house that was caused by steam from boiling water when the lightning strike occurred. The damaged piping was never dug up but a new replacement line was laid next to the old one restoring water to the insured. For Coverage A, I know that the insurance company has the duty to prove that the damage is from something excluded in the HO3. However it is the insured's duty to provide the damaged property for inspection under the Conditions #2 Your Duties After Loss. Please advise if it is the insurance company's responsibility to cover the excavation costs up front so that we can access the damaged property for inspection or is it the Insured's responsibility to pay the excavation costs up front and we reimburse if the claim is determined to be covered?

Maryland Subscriber

Am I correct that the insured is claiming a lightning strike hit the underground pipe and ruptured it? If so, then you can easily verify whether there was a storm in the area that day, and where lightning hit by using an outside vendor (I think it's called "Strikefax", appropriately enough). If you don't want to take that route, then here are your options: a) you would have to prove (by excavating the pipe) that lightning was not the cause; or b) point out that the insured must "show the damaged property" (condition 2.f.(1)), which he has failed to do. But at this point, the insured could state that he is also required to "protect the property from further damage," and "If repairs to the property are required, [he]

13

must (1) Make reasonable and necessary repairs to protect the property." So, the insured did make reasonable repairs by replacing the pipe.

Under the 1991 HO 00 03, the argument can be made that water is personal property, and the lightning strike caused the loss of personal property. So, the repairs undertaken to restore the personal property would be covered. (I'm not sure about your comment on the steam from boiling water; did that cause any damage to the structure?) The 2000 HO 00 03 specifically states that water and steam are not covered property.

Bottom line, since there are strong arguments on the part of the insured, and fewer on your side, I think you would have to get documentation as to lightning strikes if you decide not to cover the claim.

Rusted and Leaking Hot Water Heater

The policyholder has water damage under a Form 3. The water heater was in a closet in the hallway and the tank rusted out as they do, and water then came out of the tank and damaged the subfloor, with eventual damage to three rooms adjacent to the hall closet. Your analysis of Open and General Perils of September 2000 approaches this set of facts but does not exactly answer the coverage question. You find coverage for the undetected loss-wet rot that is within walls or floors and ceilings caused by repeated seepage... as an exception to the mold, fungus, or wet rot exclusion. You also appear to find coverage for a pipe which wears out and begins to leak, or better said, the damage which results from that. Would you distinguish if it was a slow leak from the water heater which remained undetected for a long period of time or would you also find coverage for that damage?

Maine Subscriber

While there is probably coverage for the loss you describe (assuming no exclusions apply, such as the insured's failure to take appropriate action to prevent further damage), there are too many variables to blanket-address a "what-if" situation.

For example, the AAIS homeowners forms specifically eliminate coverage for loss caused by repeated seepage and leakage, while the unendorsed ISO 2000 forms cover a loss if it is hidden within walls or between floors. However, having said that, many carriers now add the limited fungi, wet or dry rot, or bacteria coverage endorsement (ISO HO 04 27, for example), which limits coverage to either the amount selected by the insured, or what the insurer will allow.

Constant/Repeated Leakage or Hidden Leaks?

An insured has an attic that is accessible by either pull down stairs or a scuttle hole in a ceiling. They do use the attic to store some seasonal items - Christmas decorations, etc, and go up there a couple of times a year to retrieve and restore these items. They go up there recently and discover mold on the roof sheathing. In one case there is no other water damage. In another case, they had discovered water leak on a ceiling which caused them to investigate. No roof shingles are missing in either case, but the roofs are both old and in need of replacement due to age. The HO0475 adds paragraph 2.e.9 which says we don't insure for loss caused by constant or repeated seepage or leakage of water, or the presence of condensation of humidity, moisture or vapor, over a period of weeks, months or years unless the resulting damage is unknown to all insured's and hidden within the walls or ceilings, or beneath the floors or above the ceilings of a structure.

Would this damage be considered hidden or unknown?

Illinois Subscriber

Yes, I believe both resulting mold damage situations are covered. The mold damage resulting from the leakage (from the roof's being worn out) and the possible humidity (where mold was found on the roof sheathing) was hidden in that it was in an area not ordinarily visible to the insureds. And, the fact that it was in the attic made it "above the ceiling."

Snow Melt, Number of Occurrences and Surface Water

We have a policyholder with water damage under a Form 3. Considerable snow built up on his roof and he pulled it down with a rake and it piled against his wall. Water melted from the snow pile and came in through his siding, damaging a side wall and the floor sheathing. The company raises questions of the water possibly being surface water and there is more than one incident of melting, with each day having a thawing and freezing cycle. It is thought that possibly additional snow that came off the roof would add to the stack, leaving the possibility of several occurrences. They also raised the possibility of lack of coverage by neglect in not removing the snow against the house, realizing that damage might occur. What are your thoughts?

New York Subscriber

The benefit of doubt must go to the insured and provide coverage for the loss. For a start, surface water is usually defined as water from rain or melting snow that meanders over the ground in no set pattern. But here, the water from the melting snow did not meander; rather, it entered the insured's dwelling from a pile of snow that melted, froze, and melted again. It would have been similar to the snow remaining on the roof and melting and being forced up under shingles and into the dwelling.

As for "additional occurrences," it appears that all loss was attributable to one pile of snow; unless the insurer can prove which exact day of melting caused which exact damage, this argument is shaky.

The exclusion for neglect links this to "at the time of loss" and failure to protect against further damage. Until the damage from the melting snow became visible, the insured did not know there was a loss and so cannot be accused of *neglect*. Obviously, once the damage became visible, the insured took the proper steps to mitigate the damage.

Damage from Ruptured Water Bed

We have a personal property claim for water damage caused by a burst water bed. Do you believe a heated water bed which bursts resulting in personal property damage is covered by either of the two following perils?

Sudden and Accidental Discharge or Overflow of Water or Steam from within a plumbing, heating, air conditioning or automatic fire protection sprinkler system, or from within a household appliance. This peril does not include loss:

a. *to the appliance or system from which the water or steam escaped;*

b. *caused by or resulting from freezing;*

c. *on the residence premises caused by accidental discharge or overflow which occurs off the residence premises.*

d. *caused by or resulting from continuous or repeated seepage or leakage of water or steam which occurs over a period of time and results in deterioration, rust, mold, or wet or dry rot;*

e. *caused by or resulting from water which backs up through sewers or drains or water which enters into and overflows from within a sump pump, well, or other type system designed to remove subsurface water which is drained from the foundation area.*

Sudden and Accidental Tearing Apart, Cracking, Burning, or Bulging of a steam or hot water heating system, an air conditioning or automatic fire protective sprinkler system, or an appliance for heating water. This peril does not include loss:

a. *caused by or resulting from freezing;*

16

b.   *caused by or resulting from continuous or repeated seepage or leakage of water or steam which occurs over a period of time and results in deterioration, rust, mold, or wet or dry rot.*

California Subscriber

Here is one where you can take your pick. There is a case in Florida, *West American v. Lowrie*, 600 So.2d 34 (Fla. App. 1992), which holds that this type of waterbed is not an appliance, and therefore there is no coverage for personal property damaged by water from it. But on the other hand, *Azze v. Hanover Insurance*, 765 A.2d 1093 (N. J. Super. 2001), states "as a matter of first impression" a heated waterbed is an appliance. However, in the latter case, the court remanded it back to the trial court.

Neither case was overturned.

So, given the legal climate of California, you might want to consider the waterbed as a household appliance. You might also (down the pike) want to get underwriting involved and offer an endorsement to buy back coverage for personal property damaged by a waterbed. That way, should a loss occur again, you can always point out that the insured could have bought coverage for this type of loss, but chose not to.

Whatever you decide to do with regard to this claim, remember you will have to be consistent if any occur in the future.

Lifting Shingles Cause Opening?

Shingles lift from wind but then go back down. Regardless of whether or not the shingle(s) reseal, does this constitute an opening to allow for interior water damage on a policy that does not provide wind-driven rain coverage.

Ohio Subscriber

The policy says that direct force of the wind must damage the building and create an opening, but it does not say the opening must be in the nature of a hole in the roof. However, because the "windstorm or hail" is a named peril, the insured must be able to prove that this was the cause of the loss. I am answering with regard to an HO 00 03, where no such restrictions apply to the dwelling coverage. For example, if water comes through a roof and soaks wallpaper and wall-to-wall carpeting, there is coverage. But for there to be contents coverage, the insured must prove the peril was the cause.

Insured Moves Friend's TV

The insured is helping owner of large plasma TV move it because it's heavy. Insured puts thumb through the screen of the TV. Is this covered or excluded under care and control?

Wisconsin Subscriber

The additional coverage would provide the only coverage, since from a liability standpoint the TV was in the insured's sole control. The other possibility would be coverage under C, but this would only apply if the insured was using the owner's TV. But, he wasn't, so, back to the additional coverage being the only recovery place. You do not state which homeowners policy is in force, but look at the coverage for "damage to property of others", an additional coverage in the liability section. This is essentially "no fault" coverage, and has always been intended to provide "good neighbor" coverage where liability need not legally be determined. Under the ISO HO 00 03 (2000 edition) there is $1,000 coverage that can be used to cover the loss.

I'm not sure the insured is legally liable for the loss, but this is a question of fact rather than of policy. For example, did the owner request the insured's help? In that case, I don't see the insured as being legally liable. After all, the insured was probably not a professional mover. Did the insured volunteer? In that case, yes, perhaps he was negligent and therefore liable. In that situation, the exclusion for "property damage to property ...in the care of an 'insured'" is not really applicable, since the property was not technically in the insured's care at all, but rather in the care of both parties doing the moving.

However, first I'd go to the additional coverage, since these questions need not be resolved to provide coverage.

Condo Policy – What are Cabinets, Coverage A or B?

In a HO 06 insurance policy, is the kitchen cabinet considered as COVERAGE A OR COVERAGE B?

West Virginia Subscriber

The standard condominium form does not contain a coverage B. Any items, such as an outside garage, that would be covered under B are covered under A.

Kitchen cabinets are covered under A: "alterations, appliances, fixtures and improvements" which are part of the building contained within the 'residence premises' [in other words, contained within the insured unit]."

However, and you didn't ask this, I know, but the place for coverage for them is contingent upon what the master condo documents call for the unit owner to insure, so they might be covered by the master policy, or by the HO-6.

Boiler Fire & HO 3 Policy

Coverage under homeowners form 3 for a boiler fire (boiler cracked because of no water and started to over heat) caused by lower water shut off failure, covered or not and is the low water shut off excluded because of failure.

Kentucky Subscriber

Although loss caused by "mechanical breakdown" is excluded, any ensuing loss not otherwise excluded is, as you point out, covered. So, the water shut off (valve?) is not covered, but the ensuing cracked boiler is (fire as the covered cause of loss).

Replacing Dwelling at Another Location

I was wondering if you have any articles or formulas regarding the settlement process requirements of an insured choosing to rebuild or purchase a replacement residence versus repairing the damages at the risk location. Specifically, I am looking as to how choosing the option of replacing property elsewhere affects the Holdback claim.

Massachusetts Subscriber

I do not know of any articles or formulas that address this situation. The standard homeowners policy allows for an actual cash value settlement to be made; once repair or replacement is complete the insurer settles the remainder of the loss. An insured can certainly elect to replace a dwelling with another at another location. The ISO 2000 HO 00 03 states that "If the building is rebuilt at a new premises, the cost described....is limited to the cost which would have been incurred if the building had been built at the original premises." If the insured purchases a different (already built) dwelling, then he or she is limited to "the necessary amount actually spent to repair or replace the damaged building."

I believe that in Massachusetts the replacement dwelling must be within the state; you would want to check the amendatory endorsement for Massachusetts.

Foreclosed Home and Fair Rental Value

We have a claim in Michigan on a DP3 policy. The actual policy is a lender force placed policy where the Bank is our insured. The Bank foreclosed on the home and the Sheriff Sale occurred on 8/8/2006. There was an extensive fire at the property on 8/26/06. In Michigan, there is a six month redemption period after the sheriff sale in which the homeowner/borrower can redeem the property.

The property in question was a rental that was vacant at the time of the fire. The policy provides coverage for Fair Rental Value. My question is would the homeowner/borrower be entitled to Fair Rental Value in this instance?

Michigan Subscriber

According to the description of fair rental value coverage, the insurer pays when the property is "rented or held for rental by [the named insured]." So, coverage depends on whether, at the time of the loss, the property was either rented or held for rental (this means that if a willing tenant showed up the bank would rent the property) by the bank. If not, there is no coverage for the bank, nor do I see coverage extending to the homeowner/borrower for this same reason. Once the sale occurred, unless the homeowner actually redeemed the property there is no reason to think he might rent it to another.

Fair Rental Value and Free Tenant

HO3- Risk is a duplex. The insured has Coverage D loss of use. She resides in one of the units & allows her mother to live in the other unit rent free. Is the insured to be reimbursed for fair rental in this circumstance?

Kentucky Subscriber

The standard HO 00 03 promises to pay fair rental value for "that part of the 'residence premises' rented to others or held for rental by [the named insured]." But in this situation, the insured allows her mother to live there rent-free; the duplex half is neither rented nor held for rental (which means available for rent). She is not out-of-pocket and providing fair rental value would go against the principle of indemnification.

Off Premises Power Failure and Damage to Property

We have an insured that is making a claim for a power surge that arose as a result of a traffic accident off the "insured location", a car struck a utility pole and caused 240 VAC to come down the 110VAC lines of the "residence premises". This caused damage to the furnace and A/C, as well as some personal property.

The adjuster handling the file says that the loss is not covered because of the Section I Exclusion 1. D which reads: "Power Failure, meaning the failure of power or other utility service if the failure takes place off the "residence premises". But, if a Peril Insured Against ensues on the "residence premises", we will pay only for that ensuing loss." According to my dictionary, a definition of failure would fit.

I remember reading an article years ago about this type of event but I can not remember the conclusion. What do you think? Is this a covered loss or not?

Ohio Subscriber

The adjuster is misreading the exclusion. It eliminates coverage for "the failure of power ... if the failure takes place off the 'residence premises'." But, in this instance, the power did not fail; rather, it intensified beyond the capability of items on the residence premises to handle it.

So, there is coverage for damage to the furnace and air conditioner, because these are parts of the dwelling, not contents.

However, in regards to personal property, it depends upon what has been damaged. The named peril which applies is "sudden and accidental damage from artificially generated electrical current, but the peril goes on to state that "this does not include loss to tubes, transistors, electronic components or circuitry that are a part of appliances, fixtures, computers, home entertainment units or other types of electronic apparatus." If the damage is therefore to the electronic components or similar items, there is no coverage.

Code Upgrade for Length of Roof Nails

On a dwelling covered by an HO3 policy form, there has recently been a code upgrade where a certain length nail has to be used; we are finding that the nails extend through to the tongue and groove of the flat roof area. Our question is would this fall under the extension of coverage, as there is no other ensuing damages caused by the nails other than the tongue and groove ceiling?

Maryland Subscriber

The 1991 ISO HO 00 03 had an amendatory endorsement giving 10% of the coverage A amount for ordinance or law. The form has since been incorporated into the 2000 edition.

The additional coverage includes coverage for increased costs incurred when ordinance or law "requires or regulates....the remodeling, removal or replacement of the portion of the undamaged part of the covered building ... necessary to complete the remodeling, repair...of that part of the covered building ... damaged by a Peril Insured Against."

So, if new nails of greater length must now be used, there is coverage. There does not need to be damage caused by the nails to the tongue and groove provided a covered cause of loss was the origin of the damage to the roof which led the roof's needing repair or replacement.

Liability for Writing Subdivision Newsletter

I have a client who writes the subdivision homeowner's newsletter. This is distributed to about 1000 residences. He has been advised by his homeowner's carrier (Cincinnati) that due to the newsletter's exposure for liability, he will be cancelled, unless he secures separate E&O liability. I had thought this liability issue had been resolved in the past and that it was automatically covered by the HO insurance. Could you advise on this issue please?

Indiana Subscriber

Normally the standard homeowners policy covers volunteer activities, but remember that liability only applies to bodily injury and property damage. Libel and slander, which would appear to be two of the most common occurrences arising out of publication of a newsletter, would have to be covered by a "personal injury" endorsement or by an umbrella. But a newsletter could also bring with it allegations of false advertising or copyright infringement, which are not covered by a personal umbrella.

You do not state if the homeowners' subdivision has a homeowners' association, but if there is one a way to handle this might be to put a liability policy (such as a CGL, which can be endorsed to include volunteers) in place and have the insured added as an additional insured.

I'm not sure why Cincinnati would want an E&O policy for the insured, although if there is a board of directors for a homeowners association the board might want one. An E&O policy would not respond to libel or slander, for example. Did the underwriter explain his or her reasoning? If so, perhaps with more information we can come up with a better solution.

Injury Occurs While Insured is Hosting Mary Kay Party

Situation: The policyholder was hosting a Mary Kay make-up party (she was not the consultant, just the host). Once the party was over and the guests were leaving, the claimant ran through the backyard back towards the house to notify another guest that they needed to move their car so she could get her car out. In the process of running in our policyholder's yard, the claimant fell injuring her ankle-damaged the tendon, received bad bruising, and sprain. Under the HO 3 edition 10 00, bodily injury arising out of or in connection with a business conducted from an insured location whether or not the business is owned or operated by insured or employs an insured is excluded. Would you consider hosting a Mary Kay make-up party a business? Our policyholder was not paid to host the party; she received free products and discounts for hosting the event.

Illinois Subscriber

I do not believe the exclusion applies in this instance for the following reasons. First, the insured did not receive anything for holding the party other than some free products and discounts. The free products are in the way of gifts; the discounts simply mean the hostess gets to spend money.

Second, the exclusion states that "'bodily injury' or 'property damage' arising out of or in connection with a 'business' conducted from an 'insured location' or engaged in by an 'insured', whether or not the 'business' is owned or operated by an 'insured' or employs an 'insured' is excluded. Looking at the wording, it is obvious that a business was not conducted from the insured premises--although business was conducted from the premises. This is a subtle distinction, I know, but is in keeping with the intention of the exclusion. Further, the insured did not own, operate, or work for the business; she simply provided a venue.

For these reasons, I believe the loss is covered. For these same reasons, medical payments coverage is available.

Musical Instruments Coverage—Business Use or Hobby?

Our Insured was driving home from a music gig when he was involved in an accident and the car caught fire. His guitar, amplifier and related accessories were in the back of the car and were destroyed by the fire. "Musician" is not the Insured's full time job, but he does play for money and his band is fairly well

known in the area. Would his equipment be considered "business property" or would this be looked upon as a hobby?

Kentucky Subscriber

The 1991 ISO is clear in that it provides only $250 for property used "at any time or in any manner" for any business purpose while away from the residence premises. So, that is the most that is available. The policy defines "business" as "trade, occupation, or profession" and does not distinguish part- from full-time employment. Most courts hold that a business means continuity and a profit motive, and that certainly fits the insured's playing for money.

The 2000 form provides broader coverage, but still, given the amount of money the insured receives, might not be adequate.

The best thing for the insured to consider is an inland marine coverage form for the instruments, which, I believe, does not eliminate coverage for business use.

Personal Auto

Rented Truck Covered Under PAP?

We have a claim where our insured rented a truck from Budget Rent-a-Truck. He mistakenly used unleaded gas instead of diesel fuel. Budget had to flush out the pipes and change the gas and engine filters. Also they used 40 gallons of gas. Their total invoice was for $798; broken down as follows:

- *$180 towing*

- *$200 road service*

- *$218 parts and material (fuel filter-$54.89; Isuzu filter-$27.32 and 40 gallons of gas-$136)*

- *$200 transport & disposal of 40 gal. gas/oil.*

- *$798 Total*

Would there be coverage under the PAP for a non-owned auto?

Would I owe for physical damage only or all the damage including the gas?

Kentucky Subscriber

The policy defines a non-owned auto as any private passenger auto, pickup van or trailer. A truck is not included in that definition and a truck with a gross vehicle weight of 25,000 can not be considered an auto. Therefore, there is no coverage for the damage to the truck.

Resident Relative Runs Out of Coverage

Our insured's brother lives with him. Brother has his own auto with minimum liability limits. Brother was in an auto accident in his own vehicle and his liability limits were exhausted. Our insured was sued under his automobile policy because the brother is considered an insured under that policy. Can our insured's auto policy be triggered under this situation?

Ohio Subscriber

While the brother (for clarification, let's call him George) is indeed an insured under your named insured's (call him Ralph) policy, exclusion B.3.a&b excludes coverage for the ownership, maintenance or use of any vehicle other than "your

25

covered auto" that is owned by any family member or available for the regular use of any family member.

Since the vehicle involved in the accident belongs to a family member, George, there is no liability coverage under Ralph's policy when George is driving George's own vehicle, even though he at times is an insured under Ralph's policy. If George had been driving Ralph's vehicle at the time of loss, then Ralph's policy would provide coverage.

The exception to the exclusion is for the named insured for the use of vehicles owned by family members; this provides coverage for the named insured, Ralph, when he is using a family member's vehicle.

Races Conducted on Parking Lot

Liability exclusion B4 and the similar exclusion 13 under part D uses the words "inside a facility designed for racing" and "organized speed contest". I compete in auto crosses that are typically done on a parking lot. A course is created with orange safety cones and it is a speed contest. There is electronic timing and the winner is the lowest time.

I think it is probably a speed contest but is it inside a facility designed for racing? What if it is not a parking lot? What if the course was set up at a race track? The final Sports Car Club of America (SCCA) event of the year is set up on a large black top area designed to be used as an auto cross area.

Pennsylvania Subscriber

You are correct to question the location of the race since the exclusion hinges on the vehicle being located inside a facility designed for racing. As the policy does not define facility designed for racing, we go to the dictionary. Merriam Webster online defines facility as something (as a hospital) that is built, installed, or established to serve a particular purpose.

While the orange cones are set up for the purpose of the race in a parking lot, it is a very temporary set up and does not fit the intent of the definition. The parking lot is used at other times for parking vehicles and that is its main purpose. Therefore, there would be coverage under the personal auto policy for the race in the parking lot.

Everything changes however when the event is moved to a race track; that definitely is a facility designed for racing, and as such any loss that may occur is excluded.

Listed Driver Able To Rent a Vehicle in Own Name?

We have the following situation with an auto policy: mom, dad and son are on the auto policy with mom and dad as the named insureds and son listed only as a driver. The son is driving one of the vehicles (titled to mom and dad) away at school and gets in an accident. Can the son rent a replacement auto in his name or does the actual named insured have to be the one to rent the vehicle. There is rental reimbursement coverage for the car but the question comes down to this: is a listed driver eligible for that coverage (to rent the vehicle) in his own name or does the named insured have to be the person to rent the car? Please advice.

Kansas Subscriber

The transportation expenses state that "we will pay....expenses not exceeding $20 a day incurred by you in the event of a loss to your covered auto." The policy (PP 00 01 01 05) defines you as the named insured shown in the declarations, and the spouse if a resident of the same household.

Therefore, a driver on the policy cannot rent a vehicle in his name and request rental reimbursement from the policy. The expenses the son may pay for the rental are not expenses of the named insured.

Certain states do have different rental provisions, so you should check to see if you have a state specific endorsement that may have different language.

Insured Backs Covered Vehicle into Relative's Company Vehicle

Fact of loss is that the insured backed into her son's company vehicle while it is parked and unoccupied. The son lives with the insured. The company vehicle is not owned by the insured or the insured's son. The son is an employee of the company.

Our auto policy has an exclusion under the liability coverage that reads: "This coverage does not apply to: .... 10.Damage to property rented to, or in the charge of, an insured person except a residence or private garage not owned by that person."

The insured's son would qualify as an insured person under the policy since he is a family member and is a resident of the household.

A claim is being brought under the insured's liability policy for the damage to the insured's son company car.

It appears that the above exclusion would apply. What is your interpretation of this exclusion?

Delaware Subscriber

We agree that the son qualifies as an insured person under the policy language, and we agree that the damage to the son's work vehicle is excluded. While the policy does not define "in the charge of" Merriam Webster online defines "in charge" as: having control or custody of something. The son does indeed have control or custody of his employer's vehicle.

Vehicle Purchased for Daughter out of Household in Parent's Name

We have an insured that purchased a vehicle for her adult daughter to drive. The adult daughter does not live with her mother. The daughter is named as a driver under the policy. The daughter is therefore driving the vehicle with permission, however, it is not occasional use it is full time use. Does the policy make a distinction between occasional permissive use and full time use? Also does the daughter have liability coverage under the policy? (We realize that the daughter would not have coverage for a temporary substitute such as a rental car.)

Kentucky Subscriber

The daughter who lives elsewhere meets the definition of insured in part B.2. of the liability insuring agreement of the policy (PP 00 01 01 05). The definition of insured includes "Any person using "your covered auto". The policy does not differentiate between occasional permissive use and full time use. If the daughter is using the vehicle with permission, she is considered an insured and liability coverage applies.

Coverage for Others Attacked While in the Insured's Vehicle

Other people are attacked and injured while in the insured auto. Is Medical Payments available to them?

Ohio Subscriber

Medical payments provide coverage for medical expenses because of bodily injury caused by an accident and sustained by an insured. The definition of insured includes you, any family member or other person while occupying a motor vehicle; occupying is defined as in, upon, getting in, on, out or off the vehicle. The policy does not define accident; therefore we go to the dictionary. Merriam Webster online defines accident as an unforeseen and unplanned event or circumstance. Certainly being attacked in the vehicle fits that definition.

Therefore, coverage exists based on our analysis, barring any policy exclusions that may apply.

Dead Deer in Roadway—Collision or Other than Collision?

Our insured struck a deer wrapped in a tarp lying on the roadway. One can argue comp or collision would apply. Per ISO form PP 00 01 other than collision coverage applies when there is "contact with a bird or animal". Included in the definition of animal in Webster's is the following language "any of a kingdom (Animalia) of living things including many-celled organisms and often many of the single-celled ones", one could argue that comp would not apply as the animal is no longer living and therefore becomes an object. One could also argue that the policy is somewhat ambiguous and this would still be contact with an animal. What is the opinion of FCS?

Maryland Subscriber

The policy states that loss with a bird or animal is considered an "other than collision" loss, and it does not state that the animal must be in any particular condition, dead or alive. Therefore we consider any animal, dead or alive, to be an "other than collision" loss. While your animal was wrapped in a tarp and may have fallen from a vehicle, most animals get into the road to begin with by being animals and unpredictable in their behavior, and while a dead animal is not nearly as unpredictable, it is still an animal nonetheless, even when it's wrapped up.

Contact with Deer then Ditch—Collision or Other than Collision?

Our insured states he was going slow and bumped a deer which then caused him to drive into a ditch. Our CRSP shops states that there is no evidence of a deer hit. The insured wants it covered under Other than Collision and the adjuster feels it should be collision due to no animal evidence.

Virginia Subscriber

The insured made contact with the animal first, which is a comprehensive loss. The contact with the deer is what caused the insured to drive into the ditch causing damage to the vehicle. The resultant damage is therefore directly related to the contact with the animal, which makes it a comprehensive loss, even though there is no visible evidence to support the insured's statement.

However, some companies do have a standing practice of considering damage collision unless there is tangible evidence (fur, blood) of contact with an animal in an effort to control fraudulent losses.

Other Than Collision Causes of Loss

The standard ISO Personal Auto Policy in Part D, damage to your auto is distinguished by either "other than collision" or "collision". Collision is defined and ten types of loss are specifically described as other than collision.

Understandably damage from missiles, falling objects, birds, animals and glass breakage is differentiated. Why are there other types of loss purposely annotated, when obviously not collision. What effect does this have on the concept of "all risk coverage" [subject to exclusions] for other than collision losses or is covered damages limited only to those listed?

Maine Subscriber

The other types of loss are annotated to give a broad example of what else could be considered an "other than collision" loss. Coverage is not limited to those ten items. If a loss is not excluded and does not meet the definition of a "collision" loss coverage is available under "other than collision".

Car Wash Arm and Radio Antenna—Collision or Other Than Collision?

I have a claim where the insured had vehicle washed at car wash and forgot to turn off radio and antennae was left up. Vehicle is controlled by the car wash and was in the stopped position when the arm came down on the vehicle to start to wash it when the antennae broke off.

Would you consider this a falling object and offer coverage under the comprehensive portion of the policy or collision as an impact with an object. Your assistance would be appreciated?

Oklahoma Subscriber

The policy does not define falling, so we go to the dictionary. Merriam Webster online defines falling as to descend freely by the force of gravity; that is not the situation here. The arm of the car wash was moving downwards normally as part of its function; the antenna was hit not because of any malfunction of the machine, but the insured forgetting to turn off the radio. If the radio had been turned off, the arm would not have made contact with the antenna; the arm was not falling but descending to perform its function. We consider this to be a collision loss.

Bodily Injury Coverage for a Named Insured

We have been informed by one of our companies that there is a potential auto liability BI claim for an insured's wife. The insured, driver of vehicle in an "at-fault" accident in which the wife, passenger, was seriously injured. The wife is also listed as a "named insured" on the PAP. We have been informed that there is no exclusion for the wife presenting a BI claim against her husband. Is this possible? Can a "named insured" pursue BI against another "named insured" and it possibly be covered under the PAP?

Indiana Subscriber

The current ISO auto policy PP 00 01 01 05 provides liability coverage for which an insured is legally responsible because of an auto accident. While there are exclusions for intentional injury or intentional property damage, and exclusions of damage to property owned by the insured, there is no exclusion for injuries to named insureds. At first glance this seems to conflict with the medical payments coverage, and it does in that duplicate payments are excluded. An insured can make a claim for injuries under both liability and medical payments as long as the identical losses are not claimed. For example, if an insured is severely injured and incurs $14,000 in medical bills and their med pay coverage limit is $5,000 the remaining $9,000 may be claimed under the liability coverage. However, the amount that was paid under medical payments cannot also be claimed under the liability coverage.

Medical payments coverage is specifically for the insured; this provides the option of leaving the liability limits available to other parties injured as a result of the accident. If the insured is involved in a large loss, it makes more sense for the insured to leave the liability coverage available for another party who could possibly sue and use the medical payments coverage for himself/family members.

However, if the insured runs into a tree causing severe injuries to a family member and expenses are above the medical payment limits, it makes sense

for the claim to be filed under bodily injury. While it is seldom seen the policy does allow it. The insured cannot collect for the identical expenses under both coverages.

✳ Ownership, Titles, and Insurable Interest

Our insured is the named insured on his personal auto policy. He has two sons that live with him one 18 and the other 20. The 20 year old has a car titled in his name and it is listed as a covered auto on our named insureds policy. I've been told that because title is held in the 20 year olds name, he must have his own insurance. Why? I see under exclusion B3 there is no liability coverage for any vehicle, other than "your covered auto" which is owned by another family member. But "your covered auto" is defined as "any vehicle shown in the declarations. So, despite ownership status, there is coverage despite the title being in the son's name, correct? Why can't each of the sons own their own car and still have them on their father's policy as long as they are living in the same household?

Maryland Subscriber

The issue you have is one of insurable interest. If the son's vehicle is titled in the son's name only, which it looks like it is, then the father has no insurable interest in the vehicle. Insurable interest is when someone stands to lose financially by the loss or damage to any given property. The vehicle being titled in the son's name indicates that the son owns the property and therefore stands to lose if the property is destroyed. The son can sell or give away the property as he sees fit, and if the vehicle is stolen, the son should receive payment as it is titled in his name. Even if the father helped pay for the vehicle, if his name is not on the title, he has no legal claim to the property.

Insurance is the transfer of risk and is designed to restore the insured to where they were before the covered property was damaged or destroyed. As the father does not own the vehicle, he cannot insure the vehicle. Property must be owned by the insured for there to be a reason to insure it. It's like me putting your vehicle on my policy; it's titled to you, not me, and I have no financial interest in the property; why then should I be able to collect financially if your vehicle is damaged?

Even though the sons live in the household with the father, what would happen if a claim check were issued to the father only, as he's the named insured on the policy? The son would not receive payment for property that is rightfully his, and the father would make money off of property that he does not own. The father could take the check to Dover and spend it at the races, leaving the son without a vehicle or compensation.

Most carriers make claim payments to the named insured, not any insured on the policy. As the named insured in this situation does not own the vehicle, claims will not issue a check if the vehicle is damaged; even though they are relatives in the same household, it is the son's property, not the father's, but it is the father's insurance policy. Even if the son contributes to the premium payment, unless he is listed as a named insured with the father on the policy, there is no coverage. Family arrangements for payments of cars and insurance do not change the legal contract of an insurance policy or a title to a vehicle.

In your situation the father is insuring something he does not own, and that violates the basic principal of insurance. I'm surprised it even got added to the policy and through underwriting, it's common for underwriting to catch the discrepancy and refuse to add the vehicle titled in someone other than the named insured's name. The son needs to have his own policy, or the father needs to be added to the title to the son's vehicle. That would give the father an interest in the vehicle he could then insure. Companies frequently will not list unmarried named insureds unless both individuals are titled to all vehicles on the policy; it depends on the company and their underwriting policy.

Subrogation and Liability Limits

Our insured was at fault for an accident. The claimant received payment from his carrier under his medical payments coverage, and that carrier is now subrogating against us for those funds. When the subrogation payment is made for that Medical Payments coverage, will that reduce the available liability limits?

Ohio Subscriber

Yes, the payment that you are being subrogated for which you will pay under your insured's liability limits does reduce the overall liability limits of the policy. It is just as if you were paying the claimant directly for the loss. If the claimant had not gone through his carrier to be paid, you would be settling directly with the claimant. The fact that the payment is generated by a subrogation claim does not change that fact that it is a legitimate claim against your policy.

Medical Payments Coverage and Other Insurance Clause

The clause reads as follows:

If there is other applicable auto medical payments insurance we will pay only our share of the loss. Our share is the proportion that our limit of liability bears to the total of all applicable limits. However, any insurance we provide with respect to a vehicle you do not own shall be excess over any other collectible auto insurance providing payments for medical or funeral expenses.

Issue: The named insured has two separate policies, each with $2,000 coverage. The insured was a passenger in a not at fault auto whose carrier provided $2,000 in medical payment coverage. The insured is injured, and incurred over $13,000 in medical bills.

Based on the med pay "other insurance" clause, the insured will first receive $2,000 from the auto carrier, where he or she was a passenger. (The insured policy deems this to be the first layer, since the insured was in a non-owned vehicle)

The insured now presents a med pay claim to the carrier for additional med pay under both auto policies. Each policy has $2,000 in med pay coverage. Since both policies have the same identical "other insurance" provisions, both amounts will have to be pro-rata as follows:

We will first combine the total available med pay limits which would be $4,000. This amount is pro-rata at 50%, thus providing $2,000 in total med pay coverage. Each policy will share in the loss by paying $1,000 each towards the medical expenses incurred by the insured.

Question: Is this analysis proper in accordance with the policy provisions, "Our share is the proportion that our limit of liability bears to the total of all applicable limits", or would the insured be entitled to $2,000 from each policy? If this analysis is incorrect, then please provide an example based on the provision.

Indiana Subscriber

Your policy language states that "our share is the proportion that our limit of liability bears to the total of all applicable limits". All applicable limits include the $2000 from the policy of the vehicle the insured was riding in. Therefore, the total available med pay limit is $6,000, not $4,000. As each policy involved has limits of $2000, each policy's proportion of the loss is 33.33%. Therefore, as the insured's policies add up to 2/3 of the coverage available, they will pay 2/3 of the loss, or a total of $4,000.

Rodent Damage to Wiring Harness

The insured vehicle was parked and would not start. The vehicle was taken to a repair facility and informed that a rodent had damaged the wiring harness. Insured reported the loss under his Personal Auto policy. There was no other damage to the vehicle.

Under the "other than collision coverage", I believe there is no coverage for the damage to repair the wiring harness based on Exclusion (2) (c); We will not pay for; mechanical or electrical breakdown or failure.

Position is based on the fact there was no other damage flowing from the damage.

Colorado Subscriber

The cause of the loss wasn't mechanical breakdown or failure; it was the contact with the rodent's teeth/claws that damaged the wiring harness causing it to no long function. Mechanical or electrical breakdown is when a part of the vehicle breaks or malfunctions without the intervention of something else. If the wiring harness had simply quit working, that would be mechanical breakdown or failure. Had the rodent not chewed on the wiring harness, it would have continued to work. Therefore, the rodent is the direct cause of loss and this therefore is an other than collision loss.

Lack of Supervision as a Cause of Loss

Our insured exited her vehicle and opened the rear driver's side door to get her 3.5 yr old grandson out of his car seat. As she did, she dropped her cell phone in the street. She got her grandson out and he went between her and the door to the front of the car. With the back door still open (into the one-way roadway with parking on the right) she bent down to pick up her cell phone. The grandson then ran into the roadway and was struck by a passing motorist. Is her negligent supervision the result of her ownership, maintenance, or use of the auto and covered by her auto policy or is it just negligent supervision and covered by her homeowner's policy?

Kentucky Subscriber

In asking about negligent supervision you're really asking a legal opinion which we cannot provide.

The insured was not maintaining the vehicle when the accident occurred, and a case could be made that picking up a cell phone outside the vehicle does not constitute an activity arising out of the use or ownership of the vehicle. If the insured and grandson were walking along the sidewalk and she dropped the phone and the child ran into the street, you have the same supervision issue. However since the door was open and if perhaps the opening of the door caused the insured to drop her cell phone it could be considered "use" of the vehicle and covered under the auto policy.

The ISO HO 03 states that liability coverage is provided for injury due to an occurrence, and occurrence is defined as accident. If it is determined that the vehicle was not in use at the time of the accident there is coverage under the homeowners form.

However, the driver of the oncoming vehicle is the one who struck the child with the vehicle, not the insured. Drivers have a duty to watch for pedestrians as well as other traffic.

Damage to Camper Discovered Several Months After Date of Loss

The policyholder has a '01 Wild Traveler camper. In the spring of 2005, the policyholder pulled his camper out from under some trees and a branch hit the camper roof. Unknown to the policyholder, there was hole in the roof and this caused rain, snow etc. to get inside the camper. The policyholder never checked to see if any damage was done to the camper roof.

There is mold damage, insulation damage, and wood damage along with interior damage. Is there only coverage for the initial roof damage or is there also coverage for the resulting damage?

Vermont Subscriber

The damage to the interior of the camper is direct and accidental damage as a result of the contact with the tree branch that caused the hole in the roof. The insured had no way of knowing that the camper was damaged, and therefore both the interior damage and the damage to the roof should be covered.

Inherent Defect

Our policy contains and exclusion for inherent defect. This term is widely misused. We have several different definitions of this term and are confused when we should use it. We were told that it was for things such as rust that naturally occur in metal. The policy states:

Under Part D - Coverage for Damage to Your Covered Auto

Exclusions:

A. We will not pay for:

    1. Loss or damage caused by insects or vermin; inherent defect; dampness, mildew, mold, rot or rust; temperature extremes; mechanical or electrical breakdown or failure; wear and tear; gradual deterioration; or loss of use.

Inherent defect is not defined in our policy. As I said there are so many different definitions of the term in different dictionaries. It is difficult to determine how to apply to insurance.

We currently have a claim for a vehicle that has damage from it raining.

Per our appraiser the paint was of low quality and failed. Would we be able to use inherent defect for this? or is it defined as things that "naturally" happen?

Georgia Subscriber

Indeed, when the policy does not define terminology, the general dictionary is the next stop. If you have varying definitions, the one that is most generous is the one that should be used.

In a confusing situation as you have here, what you want to do is look at the language and also look at the basic intent of the policy. Merriam Webster online defines inherent as: involved in the constitution or essential character of something; belonging by nature or habit. Defect is defined as an imperfection that impairs worth or utility. Your definitions may or may not be similar.

Looking at your exclusion, the policy intent is to not pay for loss from the inherent defect itself. In your situation, the paint was defective; therefore your policy will not pay to repaint the car because of the defective paint. However, the water damage is separate from the defect- it is a result of water that was allowed to get to exposed areas because the paint was defective. The area was exposed due to the defect, but the cause of the loss to the affected area was the water.

Likewise, if a rat had chewed a hole in a hose there would be no coverage to repair the hose; however, if the damaged hose had started a fire, there would be coverage. The rat caused the hole, but not the fire.

Waiver of Deductible

We received a claim for our insured - they backed out of their garage and into their parked insured vehicle. Under the PA00 02 personal auto policy Part D - Coverage for Damage to your Auto, there is a section for Waiver of Collision Deductible. The section in question reads: We will waive the entire deductible shown in the Declarations for collision of your covered auto with: B. Another vehicle insured by us or by any of our affiliated companies. This waiver of collision deductible (B.) shall not apply if we or any of our affiliated companies have waived a deductible on any other vehicle involved in the collision that is owned by or furnished or available for the regular use of you or any family member.

With this language, even though this may not be the intent, I read that because there were two Westfield Insured vehicles involved, and we are not waiving a deductible (because damages to one of the vehicles is under deductible amount, or they are not claiming the damages to one of the vehicles) that we waive the deductible for the vehicle that is being claimed for damage. In other words :Two insured vehicles involved, waiver of deductible for one being repaired as there is no other deductible being waived because the other is not being claimed. Can you please let me know how you read into this coverage?

Ohio Subscriber

In the situation you present, the first deductible is not really waived; if the damage is below the deductible amount and therefore the insured receives no payment, the deductible has actually been applied. If the damage is not claimed at all by the insured then again, the deductible is not waived, there is no claim being made.

Since you have not waived one deductible, and the policy indicates that the waiver does not apply if a deductible has already been waived, not applied, then in our opinion you are correct and should waive the deductible on the other vehicle.

Commercial Lines

COMMERCIAL GENERAL LIABILITY

Additional Insured Covered for Claim by Employee of Named Insured?

The CGL form is endorsed by CG 20 26, additional insured—designated person or organization. Is there coverage for the additional insured under the CGL form of the named insured if an employee of the named insured makes a claim against the additional insured?

Oklahoma Subscriber

CG 20 26 makes an additional insured of the person or organization shown in the schedule with respect to liability arising out of the named insured's operations or premises. If that is the basis for this claim, there is no exclusion on the CGL form that would prevent coverage for the additional insured. You may be thinking about the employers liability exclusion, but that applies to the situation of employer and employee. Since the employee in your scenario is not the employee of the additional insured, the exclusion does not apply.

Due to the separation of insureds clause on the CGL form, the insurance applies separately to each insured against whom a claim is brought. This makes the additional insured a separate insured from the named insured, and so, the claim by an employee of the named insured against the additional insured is not going to be affected by the employers liability exclusion.

Bodily Injury Defined

One of our clients has a radiology laboratory. A patient that visited the lab for radiology services was told by a technician to remove his clothes and put on a robe. Right after this, the technician grabbed the patients genitals without saying a word. Now this patient is suing our insured, the owner of the lab. Would this claim be covered under the CGL form?

Florida Subscriber

No, the CGL form applies to bodily injury or property damage. Bodily injury is defined on the policy as bodily injury, sickness, or disease sustained by a person, including death resulting from any of these at any time. So, unless the patient suffered some actual bodily injury as defined on the CGL form, there is not going to be any coverage under the CGL form for this claim. This sounds more like sexual harassment or molestation and unless these actions are

accompanied by bodily injury, the CGL form does not cover claims arising from them.

The insured may want to review his professional liability policy to see if such a claim would be covered under that policy.

Care, Custody, or Control Exclusion and the Insured

I have a question regarding the CGL exclusion for damage to personal property in the care, custody, or control of the insured. Our insured is a water remediation company that removes and stores property that has been water damaged, and then has an employee return the property after it has been cleaned. At that point, the homeowner claims that not all the property has been returned by the employee and brings an action against the company, the named insured; no employees are named in the lawsuit. The insurer denies coverage due to the care, custody, or control exclusion.

Does the exclusion apply to the named insured?

California Subscriber

The care, custody, or control exclusion applies only to the particular insured who has the personal property in his care, custody, or control at the time of the loss or damage. The CGL form recognizes the separation of insureds and so, the named insured is a separate insured from the employee. This means that the phrase "the insured" refers to that particular insured that has the care, custody, or control of the property at the time of loss. In your scenario, the named insured did not have the care, custody or control-the employee did and so, the exclusion does not prevent coverage for the named insured should he be held liable for the damage. If the exclusion used the phrase "your care, custody, or control", or the phrase "care, custody, or control of any insured", then the named insured here may have a coverage problem. But, that was not the language used. The phrase used was "the insured", which makes the exclusion applicable to just that particular insured who has the care, custody, or control of the property at the time of loss.

Furthermore, the CGL form declares in the who is an insured clause that an employee is not considered to be an insured for property damage to property in his care, custody, or control. Therefore, the employee is not an insured at all for a loss that involves property damage to property in his care, custody, or control, and since that is the case, no insured really has the care, custody or control over the property. This makes the exclusion irrelevant to your scenario.

Claims-Made Policies and Bodily Injury Claim

From 1974 to 1997, the claimant was exposed to petroleum products as the lessee of a gas station franchise owned by our insured. The claimant developed a transitional cell carcinoma of the kidney, allegedly caused by the prolonged exposure to the petroleum products sold in the gas station. Although the claimant did not specify when the carcinoma began or manifested itself, on September 8, 2005, he acknowledged that the carcinoma could have been caused by the exposure to the chemicals.

The existing policies are two claims-made policies, one with a policy period of January 1998 to January 1999, and the other with a policy period of December 2005 to December 2006. Both policies have a retroactive date of 1988. The complaint against the insured was filed and reported in November 2006. Could this claim be denied in its entirety because the exposure to the chemicals began before the retroactive date?

Puerto Rico Subscriber

Claims-made policies will not apply to bodily injury or property damage that occurs before the retroactive date, but the main thing about a claims-made policy is that the claim has to be made during the policy period, or any extended reporting period. So, since you have two claims-made policies here, you should first see if the claims were made during the policy periods or any extended reporting periods. If not, the retroactive date is not relevant to coverage. If the answer is yes, then you can proceed to the issue of whether the injury or damage occurred before or after the retroactive date.

The answer to that question depends on how your jurisdiction views when injury occurs. There are four general theories accepted by courts as to when injury occurs. The exposure theory, the manifestation theory, the triple trigger theory, and the injury in fact theory are the ones in vogue today, and a coverage depends on which theory your particular jurisdiction accepts. You should contact an attorney who is familiar with the law in your jurisdiction to see which theory applies in such a case as this.

As an example, though, the exposure theory holds that when the disease manifests itself has nothing to do with when the bodily injury occurred. Liability coverage is triggered by the victim's exposure to the harm-causing agent. So, in your case, the injury occurred in 1974, or before the 1988 retroactive date.

As another example, in the manifestation theory, the date of the actual diagnosis of the disease determines the date of occurrence. So here, the date of September 2005 may be the date, and that would involve both your policies.

Basically, you need two items here: find out what theory of injury your jurisdiction follows, and see if the claim was made during the policy periods or extended reporting periods. The answers will help to decide about denials of or acceptance of coverage. It would be more appropriate all around if these items were clear before any denial of coverage is made.

Completed Operations Claim and Damage to Work Exclusion

Our insured is a carpenter. Over the past few years, he has done several jobs for the claimant. One of those jobs was to replace the floor in the claimant's kitchen. The latest job was to replace several cabinets in the kitchen. Several weeks after the cabinet job was finished, one of the cabinets fell, damaging the wall to which it was attached. The falling cabinet also damaged the cabinet that was installed next to it by our insured. And, the floor was also damaged by the falling cabinet. It was determined that the cause of the falling of the cabinet was the bolts pulling away from the stud used by the insured in the installation.

The questions pertain to all of the damage. Is a claim for the cabinet that fell and was damaged covered? Is the damaged wall covered? The other cabinet? The floor? The question about the floor is especially interesting since it is the insured's work even though it was done under a different contract and at a different time from the cabinet work. What are your thoughts?

Ohio Subscriber

This is a completed operations claim since the damage clearly occurred after the work of the insured was finished. And, the exclusion on the CGL form that might apply to this claim situation would be exclusion l., damage to your work.

There is no question as to coverage for the damage to the wall. The wall was not the work of the insured. The insured's work caused damage to the wall, another's property. This type of claim is what the CGL form was meant to cover.

As for the damage to the cabinets, both the one that fell and the one that was damaged by the falling cabinet, exclusion l. would apply. Both cabinets were put up by the insured and would fall into the category of the named insured's work, that is, work performed by the named insured and materials furnished in connection with such work. The property damage to that work arose out of the work of the insured and it fits the definition of the products-completed operations hazard as found in the CGL form. These points are all part of exclusion l. and make that exclusion applicable to this claim.

As for the floor damage, applying exclusion l. would be something of a stretch. The exclusion says that there is no coverage for property damage to the work of the named insured arising out of the work. Narrowly reading this exclusionary language, this means that the property damage has to arise out of the actual work done on the property by the insured. In other words, if the floor damage arose out of the work that the insured did on the floor, that is within the scope of the exclusion. But since, the damage to the floor did not arise out of the insured's work on the floor, but on the cabinets (which are a separate piece of work entirely), exclusion l. does not extend that far.

The damage to the floor and to the wall should be covered by the insured's CGL policy.

Damage to Property Exclusions and the Work of the Named Insured

We have an insured who is an electrical contractor. He was installing wiring for an alarm system in a new house. Part of the wiring had to go through the window frame. Apparently there are only certain locations one can drill through the frame safely and not compromise the window's integrity. In this particular case, the insured drilled through the window frame in the wrong place. The window was already installed by another contractor.

Due to the location of the holes our insured drilled, the builder claimed that the manufacturer's warranty on the windows was voided, and he demanded that our insured replace all of the windows in the house that he had worked on. The insurer is denying the claim based on exclusion j6, that particular part of any property that must be restored, repaired, or replaced because the named insured's work was incorrectly performed on it. We are wondering if this is applicable since the insured was not installing the windows, just wiring around the windows. Wouldn't the insured's work simply be the wiring?

Ohio Subscriber

Exclusion j6 on the CGL form pertains to property that was damaged and has to be repaired because the named insured's work was incorrectly performed on it. In this case, the insured was there to wire the house and the work of the insured was not the windows; the windows were merely incidental to the purpose of the insured's work. Exclusion j5 would be the more appropriate exclusion to apply.

This exclusion states that there is no coverage for property damage to that particular part of real property on which the named insured is performing operations if the property damage arises out of those operations. The insured in this case was performing operations on the window and the damage arose out of those operations. The windows were not the object of the insured's work, but he certainly was performing operations, or working, on the windows when he caused the damage.

Moreover, if the claim is just that the warranty has been voided, that is not really property damage as defined on the CGL form. Property damage is physical injury to tangible property and loss of use of tangible property. A voided warranty is not physical injury, not a loss of use of property, and definitely not tangible property.

So, either through exclusion j5 or due to lack of property damage, there is no coverage for this claim against your insured.

Damage to Your Product Exclusion on the CGL Form

We have a client that lays hardwood flooring. He was hired to install hardwood flooring in a model home and this was finished with no problems. After awhile, the builder of the home was getting ready to sell the home and asked our client to refinish the flooring due to heavy traffic causing severe scuffing to the floor. The insured did this work and was moving the refrigerator back into place when the water line developed a leak. This was not noticed by anyone at the time and the water damaged the flooring. The whole section of the flooring has to be replaced.

The insurer of our client is denying coverage, saying that the flooring is the product and the work of the insured, and the damage to product and work exclusions on the CGL form preclude any coverage for the damage claim. We don't agree with this denial of coverage and would appreciate your review of this situation.

New Jersey Subscriber

The damage to your product exclusion is not applicable in this situation. "Your product" is a defined term in the CGL form and it does not include real property. When the flooring was put down, it became part of the home, it became real property. So, any damage to the flooring would not be considered damage to the product of the named insured.

The damage to your work exclusion applies if the damage to that work itself arose out of the work. As you describe this occurrence, the damage to the floor was due to the water leak and not because of any work that the insured did on the floor. It is not relevant in an event such as this that the flooring was work done by the insured in the past. The damage did not arise out of that past work.

The insurer is not reading the exclusions properly in this event. If the insured caused the water leak because of his negligently moving the refrigerator, the work of the insured caused damage to another's property and this is what the general liability policy is meant to cover.

Employee Benefits Liability Coverage Applies to Stolen Funds?

Our insured has a CGL form and an endorsement, CG 04 35, employee benefits liability coverage. Our insured provided funds to an outside investment firm on behalf of his employees. The investment firm allegedly stole the funds. The insured then used his own money to replace the funds with another investment firm and is now looking to the insurer to reimburse him for the loss.

We don't see any coverage for the claim under the CGL firm, but we were wondering if there is coverage under the endorsement. Specifically, we want to know if the actions of the insured fall within the administration of the employee benefit program. The insured should have performed due diligence in his placing of the investment funds and we wonder if his alleged failure to perform this due diligence is improper administration. What do you think?

Ohio Subscriber

CG 04 35 is not going to provide coverage for the insured in this instance.

The coverage under the terms of this endorsement is for the negligent administration of the employee benefit program. Administration is a defined term on CG 04 35. It means: providing information to employees with respect to eligibility for or scope of employee benefit programs; handling records in connection with the program; or effecting, continuing, or terminating any employee's participation in the program. None of these parts to the definition describe your insured's actions (or omissions). An outside firm allegedly stole the funds. That is not the insured providing information to employees, or handling records, or effecting or terminating any employee's participation in the program.

Moreover, CG 04 35 has a clause describing the duties of the insured in the event of an act or omission that the insured will not, except at his own cost, voluntarily make a payment, assume any obligation, or incur any expense without the consent of the insurer. When the insured used his own money

to replace the lost funds without the consent of the insurer, he breached the insurance contract. That means that the insurer has a right to void the contract and deny coverage.

Failure to Supply Exclusion and General Liability Coverage

An exclusionary endorsement commonly attached to the CGL form issued to rural electric co-operatives is CG 22 50, exclusion—failure to supply. This exclusion prevents coverage for bodily injury or property damage arising out of the failure of any insured to adequately supply gas, oil, water, electricity, or steam.

What is the intent of this exclusion? Does the exclusion apply to claims that arise out of the insured's operational negligence as it administers a fully energized grid, or is the exclusion intended to exclude claims of a blackout/brownout nature? As an example, the insured co-op intends to disconnect power to a customer due to nonpayment but inadvertently disconnects the power at the wrong location, resulting in property damage to this innocent third party. Does the insured have liability coverage for this incident? Or, if the insured performs repairs or replacement work on a transformer and leaves a connection loose which results in intermittent power supply to a home, which in turn, damages electronic equipment; is this covered? Or finally, the insured invokes a rolling blackout in response to a supply and demand imbalance; if that results in a claim, does the insured have any coverage?

Indiana Subscriber

The extent of the exclusion is very broad in nature. As you note, coverage is excluded for bodily injury or property damage arising out of the failure of any insured to adequately supply gas, oil, water, electricity, or steam. Based on this wording, the examples you gave pertaining to inadvertently disconnecting the power supply or invoking a rolling blackout fit the exclusionary language. Whether the failure to supply is accidental or intentional, the exclusion applies.

CG 22 50 does have an exception pertaining to failure to supply resulting from the sudden and accidental injury to tangible property owned or used by any insured. So, in your one scenario about the insured performing repairs, if the failure to supply resulted from the insured causing sudden and accidental injury to its own property, claims resulting from the failure to supply would be covered.

In summary, each scenario has to be judged on its own details. Most of the time, the exclusion will apply, but that exception does provide a small loophole, depending on the circumstances of the event.

Faulty Work of Insured Raises Coverage Question

Our insured was hired to do a welding job. When he went to the job site, the general contractor asked him to weld a steel frame onto a countertop that had already been installed but was starting to sag. While doing this, the heat from the welding torch cracked the marble countertop. Would the damage caused to the countertop be excluded under the CGL form?

New York Subscriber

Exclusion j5 on the CGL form would apply to this property damage claim. That exclusion declares that there is no coverage for property damage to that particular part of real property on which the insured is performing operations if the damage arises out of those operations. A case can be made that the insured caused the property damage while he was working on performing operations on the countertop. After all, he was welding some steel to the underneath of the countertop. It is not as if he was welding on a table or a chair or some other part of the house and accidentally scorched the countertop. He was attaching something to the countertop and that is performing operations on the countertop.

The insured could argue that he was not there on the job site to work on the countertop; that it was only incidental to his work as a welder; that he was not working on that particular part of real property (the countertop) but was working on the steel support frame. And, if the insured had damaged the steel support that would not be covered, but any other damage he caused would be covered. However, since the insured was actually attaching the steel frame to the countertop, he was performing operations on the countertop, and the damage arose out of his faulty work. This is a situation to which the exclusion applies.

Host Liquor Liability and General Liability Coverage

I have a question regarding liquor liability. My insured operates a limousine service for weddings and other celebrations. As part of the service, the insured provides complimentary alcoholic beverages for the passengers. Does the CGL liquor liability exclusion apply in this situation and leave the insured with no coverage should an accident occur?

Connecticut Subscriber

The liquor liability exclusion on the CGL form applies if the insured is in the business of manufacturing, distributing, selling, serving, or furnishing alcoholic beverages. From the situation as you describe it, it can be said that the insured, as part of its business, does distribute or serve or furnish alcoholic beverages. In reality, this is not the insured's main business since you describe this as a limousine service, but the liquor liability exclusion does not say anything about incidental operations or complimentary services. It would be reasonable for an insurer to apply the exclusion if an accident occurred and the resulting claims were extensive. The insurer could say that part of the insured's business was distributing or serving or furnishing alcohol and so, the exclusion applies. If the issue then ended up in court, the court may disagree with this interpretation, but the dispute would still be there.

Your insured might want to consider buying a liquor liability policy, perhaps on an if any basis if an insurer would agree. That way, the insured would have liability coverage for injuries due to the insured's selling, serving, or furnishing alcoholic beverages; and the premium for the coverage would probably not be too expensive for the insured since the serving of alcohol is not an extensive part of the insured's business.

You did not ask about the auto exclusion on the CGL form, but you should be aware that this exclusion applies to bodily injury or property damage claims arising out of the ownership or use of any auto by the insured. So, even if the liquor liability exclusion is not applied to exclude coverage under the CGL form, this does not prevent the auto exclusion from being used by the insurer to exclude coverage for injuries and damages due to an accident involving the ownership or use of an auto. On the other hand, the standard business auto policy does not have a liquor liability exclusion in its provisions, so the serving or furnishing of alcoholic beverages to passengers is not relevant to a claim involving the insured's auto.

Impaired Property Exclusion Applies to Property Damage Claim

Our insured makes screws and bolts. These items are used in large signs and poles for the signs. After a certain set of signs were put in place, they were tested for stability but some did not pass the test. It was determined that the screws and bolts in these failed signs were not made to correct specifications and they will have to be extracted and replaced with different screws and bolts. There is no claim for bodily injury or property damage at this time, but we are wondering if the general liability policy will cover the cost of taking down the signs and poles and replacing the screws and bolts. Is this a property damage claim?

Michigan Subscriber

This is a property damage claim if the definition of property damage on the CGL form is met. The definition is physical injury to tangible property, including all resulting loss of use; or loss of use of tangible property that is not physically injured. However, even if property damage occurs here, the impaired property exclusion will prevent coverage for a property damage claim.

This exclusion applies to property damage to impaired property or property that has not been physically injured arising out of a defect or deficiency or inadequacy in the named insured's product. In order for the impaired property exclusion to be applied, the definition of impaired property has to be met, and that is the case here. The incorrectly made screws and bolts are the product of the named insured; they were incorporated into another's property; they made the other piece of property less useful or not useful at all; and the signs and poles can be restored to use by the removal and replacement of the defective screws and bolts. So, any claim for property damage will not be covered by the CGL form due to the impaired property exclusion.

And, the expenses for taking down the signs and poles will not be covered either because of the recall exclusion. This exclusion applies to damages claimed for any loss, cost or expense incurred by the named insured or others for the loss of use, repair, replacement, or removal of the named insured's product or impaired property, if the product or property is withdrawn or recalled from use by any person or organization because of the deficiency or inadequacy of the product or property.

Pollution Liability Coverage for Landowners

Endorsement CG 24 15 10 01, the limited pollution liability extension endorsement, is available in most states. My client owns some property that currently is leased to others and is used by them as a small grocery store; my client only owns the land and has nothing to do with the store. Would CG 24 15 give my client some pollution liability coverage under these circumstances? He is worried that he will end up paying for a pollution claim just because he owns the land.

Also, how would an underground storage tank be handled by CG 24 15? If the tenants were to put in an underground storage tank for gasoline sales, would the endorsement provide coverage for my client in the event of a pollution claim?

Colorado Subscriber

CG 24 15 replaces the pollution exclusion (f) found on the commercial general liability (CGL) coverage forms and provides limited protection, subject to a stated aggregate limit, for some on premises exposures that could face a

landowner. Under the standard CGL forms, bodily injury or property damage arising out of the dispersal or discharge of pollutants at or from any premises owned by any insured is excluded. CG 24 15 deletes this part of the pollution exclusion, thereby giving coverage to a landowner like your client. For example, if the tenant poured cleaning solvent out in back of the store and the solvent seeped into the ground and eventually damaged a neighbor's property, CG 24 15 would provide liability and defense costs coverage to the landowner.

Another part of the standard pollution exclusion that is amended by this endorsement is part f (1) (d). That part of the exclusion precludes coverage for injury or damage arising from any premises on which the insured or a contractor is performing operations if the pollutants are brought onto the premises in connection with such operations. Endorsement CG 24 15 revises this exclusionary language to apply only when the operations are to test for, monitor, clean up, remove, contain, treat, detoxify, or neutralize, or in any way respond to, or assess the effects of pollutants. So, operations by the insured that do not have as their purpose any clean up or control of pollutants, and that cause some injury or damage due to a release or discharge of pollutants, will be covered due to CG 24 15. As an example, if the landowner has a lawn care company spray the property with herbicides or insecticides, a subsequent injury or property damage claim by a neighbor against the landowner will be covered under the general liability policy.

As for the underground storage tank, the endorsement clearly states that damages and injuries based on the escape of pollutants from an underground storage tank on premises owned by any insured are not covered. Therefore, if your client allows the storage tank to be put into his land, he will face any subsequent pollution claim without the benefit of insurance coverage from the general liability policy. What you may want to consider is CG 00 42, the underground storage tank policy. This policy is a claims-made policy that provides coverage for the insured for bodily injury or property damage claims caused by an underground storage tank incident. Such an incident is defined on CG 00 42 as the release or the discharge or leak of petroleum from an underground storage tank into ground water, surface water, or subsurface soils. CG 00 42 also provides coverage for corrective action costs, sums the insured has incurred to pay for reasonable and necessary expenses in response to an underground storage tank incident; in other words, cleanup costs due to the release of petroleum from an underground storage tank. CG 00 42 is not going to pay for fines or penalties imposed by the government for a leak of pollutants, and it will not pay for the restoration or routine maintenance of any insured underground tank or of the site where any insured tank is located, but CG 00 42 does give the insured some liability coverage and defense expense coverage for claims arising due to his underground storage tank.

Incidentally, CG 24 15 does not allow coverage for any cleanup costs requested or ordered or required by the government. That part of the pollution exclusion is not modified by CG 24 15.

Med Pay Coverage for Renter?

The medical payments coverage of the CGL form has an exclusion pertaining to injury to a person who is injured on normally occupied premises. How would this apply to the following scenario?

The insured is a beauty salon that leases chairs to seven beauty stylists and nail professionals. There is no written lease agreement involved in this situation. A nail professional leaves her chair area and trips and falls over a curling iron cord near the leased chair area of another stylist. Would the exclusion apply and prevent coverage for the injured nail professional?

Tennessee Subscriber

The exclusion under the med pay coverage agreement usually refers to a tenant being injured in his own specific space that he has rented and is not meant to apply if the tenant is injured in a common area. This scenario of yours adds a lot of uncertainty since you are just talking about renting chairs and chair space. However, the med pay coverage should apply in this situation for the following reasons.

First, there is enough uncertainty and ambiguity in this scenario to create a reasonable doubt as to coverage. Any reasonable doubt has to be decided in favor of the insured and in favor of coverage.

Second, the exclusion reads "… on that part of premises … that the person normally occupies". Presumably in your scenario, the injured person did not normally occupy that part of the premises where she fell and was injured. The individual chairs were leased to individuals and that injured individual was supposed to be at the chair she leased. If she was injured at another's chair area, or another's part of the premises, that is akin to an apartment renter being injured in apartment A while he actually lives in apartment B. He does not normally occupy apartment A so the exclusion does not apply to him. Exclusions are meant to be read narrowly in scope and that means in this case, the injured person was not actually injured in the part of the premises that she normally occupies.

Third, while the insured may not be liable for this injury, it is possible that a claim or lawsuit based on liability could be filed against the insured just because of the ownership of the chairs and general premises. And while the insured may

not be held liable at all for the injury, the costs of defense will still be there. In order to forestall this expense and since med pay is not based on liability, but is there as something of goodwill coverage in order to perhaps prevent any lawsuits, it makes sense to offer the med pay for this reason alone.

In summary, the exclusion is not applicable and the med pay coverage agreement applies in this case.

Mobile Equipment under the CGL Form

Our insured is a road builder. He uses a water truck in his work to dampen the terrain to keep the dust down during road construction. The insurer wants to call this vehicle an auto, but we think it is mobile equipment to be covered for liability purposes under the CGL form. May we have your opinion?

California Subscriber

We agree in general that a water truck as you describe it could fit into the definition of mobile equipment under the CGL form.

There are at least two portions of the definition that could encompass the water truck. First, it is a vehicle "designed for use principally off public roads" since it is used to dampen the terrain at construction sites; this description is in paragraph (a) of the mobile equipment definition. The second part of the definition that applies is the part that describes a vehicle "maintained primarily for purposes other than the transportation of persons or cargo" — paragraph (f). The water truck is maintained primarily to help in the construction business of the insured and not to transport people or cargo. That is what this part of the definition is intended to cover; that is, a piece of equipment used in the business of the insured where the main liability exposure is on the construction site, not on a public road.

Note also that the section of the definition dealing with self-propelled vehicles with permanently attached equipment bolsters this construction site exposure viewpoint in that it talks of equipment designed primarily for road maintenance being considered as autos, but equipment designed for construction not being considered as autos. Your insured's water truck is used in the construction process, not for road maintenance, so it should be seen as mobile equipment.

However, the current version of the CGL form and its definition of mobile equipment can change the situation. Mobile equipment now does not include any land vehicles that are subject to a compulsory or financial responsibility law or other motor vehicle insurance law in the state where it is licensed or principally garaged. These types of vehicles are considered to be autos and if they are involved in a claim for bodily injury or property damage, the auto policy and not the CGL form is the proper coverage policy. So, if the water truck in this instance is subject to a financial responsibility law or other motor vehicle insurance law in the particular state where it is licensed or principally garaged, the insurer is correct in calling it an auto.

Ongoing Operations Claim not Covered due to Damage to Property Exclusion?

We have a question concerning the CGL form and the damage to property exclusions. Our insured was hired to do work on a house under construction. Part of his job was to pour the foundation; another contractor then was to come in and build the actual house to sit on the foundation. Another part of the insured's work was to prep the site prior to the building of the foundation. After he built the foundation, the insured was backfilling around the foundation and apparently put too much pressure on the walls and crushed the walls of the foundation. This led to claim against the insured for causing property damage.

We think this is an ongoing operations claim because the work that the insured was hired to do was not completed even though the actual work on the foundation was done. Do you agree?

And, do you think exclusion j5 would exclude coverage for damage done to the foundation? Or, would exclusion j6 apply?

Finally, if there is coverage to replace the foundation, is the cost to remove backfill from the foundation walls part of the coverage?

Pennsylvania Subscriber

This is an ongoing operation claim since the damage occurred while the insured was still performing his work. Backfilling around a foundation is part of the process for which the insured was engaged. However, the damage to property exclusions on the CGL form are not applicable in this instance.

Exclusion j5 on the CGL form applies to property damage to that particular part of real property on which the insured is performing operations, if the property damage arises out of those operations. While the insured was backfilling around the foundation, the case can be made that he was not actually working, or performing operations, on the foundation. The foundation was already poured and finished and the backfilling was a separate operation, albeit part of the insured's overall job. Moreover, the exclusion pertains to "that particular part" on which the insured is performing operations. The insured was not working on that particular part, the foundation; he was working on that particular part, the

backfilling. For this exclusion to be applicable, the insured would have had to be working on the foundation itself or would have had to damage the backfill.

Exclusion j6 on the CGL form applies to property damage to that particular part of any property that has to be repaired or restored because the insured's work was incorrectly performed on it. As you infer, the work on the foundation was not faulty; that particular part, which is the foundation, was not damaged due to faulty work being performed on it. It was damaged not because of the work on it, but because of the negligent backfilling.

This seems to be a situation wherein the insured damaged his own work by his own work, but none of the damage to property exclusions would apply due to the circumstances of the occurrence. Even the damage to your work exclusion (exclusion l.) is not applicable since that is for completed operations and the insured had not completed his work at the job site when the damage occurred.

As for the cost to remove the backfill, if the foundation can only be replaced by removing the backfill, then the removal is included in the claim charges.

Personal Injury Coverage Applies to Adverse Information?

We are handling a complaint wherein the plaintiff claims damages due to adverse information allegedly provided by our insured to the credit bureaus. Would this qualify for coverage under the personal injury liability insuring agreement as libel or slander?

Florida Subscriber

The words "libel" and "slander" are not defined in the commercial general liability (CGL) form. The dictionary defines libel as a method of defamation expressed in writing that is injurious to the reputation of another. Slander is defined as the speaking of false and defamatory words of another that causes injury to that person's reputation. And the personal injury definition under the CGL form includes oral or written publication, in any manner, of material that slanders or libels a person.

You will have to check out the facts of the situation, but usually, credit reports are in print and are not presented by speaking; that is, slander is most probably not involved here. As for this claim being one of libel, that is really a legal question that needs to be answered by an attorney; and, you should also check with an attorney on whether truth can be used as a shield against a claim of libel.

In any case, in this situation, the insured is entitled to a defense at the very least over the issue of whether this is a covered personal injury claim. If the insured is found liable due to causing personal injury, there is no exclusion on the CGL form to prevent coverage. This is presuming, of course, that the insured did not knowingly publish false information, which is an exclusion under the terms of the personal and advertising injury insuring agreement.

Pollution Exclusion and Owned Premises

Does the pollution exclusion on the CGL form eliminate coverage for bodily injury alleged as a result of pollution emanating from within a building that was never owned by the insured? The insured owned some land which he sold to the claimant. The claimant then had a house built on that land. After the home was built, it was discovered that sewer gases were escaping into the house. The source of the gas was an unsealed joint in the sewer stack in the attic of the house.

If a claim is made against the insured, would the pollution exclusion apply? The exclusion pertains to injury due to escape of pollutants at or from any premises, site, or location which is or was owned by the insured. We think that the words "site" and "location" do not denote buildings but merely refer to land or sea, and the word "premises" denotes land and the buildings on it. So, since the claim is based on pollutants emanating from the building and not the land, and the building was never owned by the insured, the pollution exclusion does not eliminate coverage. What do you think?

Pennsylvania Subscriber

This is an interesting interpretation and distinction, but we do not agree with it. It is a stretch to separate the building from the land. Both are real property and both would be sold together if the current owner wanted to sell. Both are listed as one postal address and both are valuated together for property tax purposes. If someone were to be injured walking on the land but not yet in the building, the CGL form (or the homeowners liability coverage) would apply since the insurance policies consider the land and building to be one location, site or premises for insurance purposes.

So, even though the pollution emanated from the building and not the land, the dispersal or escape of pollutants came from a location or premises once owned by the insured. If for some reason the insured is held liable for the injuries, the CGL form is not going to provide coverage because of the pollution exclusion.

Property Damage Defined

What is the meaning of "property damage?" We know what the definition says on the commercial general liability coverage forms, but we also know that lawsuits have been filed concerning whether or not a particular claim really does constitute property damage. As examples, there have been legal wrangles over the question of defining "property damage" to include diminution in value, loss of potential income, and loss to proprietary information. Now, is there some simple, certain, definitive interpretation of property damage on which we can rely so as to preclude questions over claims coverage?

Georgia Subscriber

The words and phrases of insurance forms are often subject to the vagaries of judicial interpretations; this applies even to those terms, such as property damage, that are defined on the forms.

Property damage is defined as physical injury to tangible property (including all resulting loss of use of that property) or loss of use of tangible property that is not physically injured; the key element in this definition to focus on is loss to or loss of *tangible* property. In ruling on the viability of claims in accordance with the property damage definition, courts around the country tend to zero in on whether or not damage has been done to property that is tangible (touchable or with a physical existence) as opposed to property in general (or everything which is or may be the subject of ownership). The following cases are some examples of this thinking.

In *St. Paul Fire and Marine Insurance Company v. National Computer Systems, Inc.*, 490 N.W.2d 626 (1992), a Minnesota court of appeals decided that "misappropriation of confidential proprietary information does not constitute property damage within the meaning of a commercial general liability policy." Here, the insurer asked the court to declare if it was obligated to defend and indemnify it's insured after the firm had been sued for allegedly violating a competitor's trade secrets. The court of appeals looked over the definition of property damage on the liability coverage form and decided that the taking of confidential information did not fit the definition requiring damages to tangible property; therefore, the complaint did not allege damage covered by the liability policy.

In *Selective Insurance Company v. J.B. Mouton & Sons*, 954 F.2d 1075 (1992) a United States court of appeals, applying Louisiana law, said that "neither deeding land to a partnership, constructing a building on land, nor giving land in payment of debt suggests physical injury to or destruction of tangible property; what was injured here was the owners' interests in a partnership, an intangible property, and so the liability policy need not respond to the claim."

In *The Kartridg Pak Company v. The Travelers Indemnity Company*, 425 N.W.2d 687 (1988) and in *Milgard Manufacturing, Inc. v. Continental Insurance Company*, 759 P.2d 1111 (1988), courts of appeals in Iowa and Oregon, respectively, decided that tangible property was not injured by diminution in value since there was no physical damage done; diminution in value was considered an economic loss or injury and not physical injury to tangible property. Therefore, such diminution did not come within the scope of the liability insurance policies.

Of course, a blanket statement that "diminution in value is not property damage" is not accurate. It would be better to say that, for diminution in value to be considered property damage, the loss of use part of the property damage definition on the CGL form has to be met. As an example of this point, see *Vogel v. Russo*, 613 N.W.2d 177 (Wis. 2000). In this case, the Wisconsin Supreme Court had to determine whether the general liability policy provided coverage for the diminution in value of a home due to faulty workmanship. The court said that it did not because the plaintiffs never lost use of their home, and diminution in value—even to the point of worthlessness—is not the same as loss of use under the terms of the insurance policy which, by its plain language, contemplates some sort of loss of use in fact, not merely a reduction in value. So, a purely economic loss, that is, a decline in value of the property, is not property damage as defined on the CGL form. But, a loss in the value of some property in that the property is made useless can be seen as property damage.

In *United States Fidelity & Guaranty Company v. Wilkin Insulation Company*, 578 N.E.2d 926 (1991), the Illinois supreme court said that "asbestos fiber contamination constitutes physical injury to tangible property"; the claim did state a case for property damage that was potentially within the scope of the policy.

There may also be a question as to whether a loss caused by conversion or disappearance is property damage; after all, with missing tangible property, the insured has suffered a loss of use of that property. As for conversion, virtually every court to consider the question has agreed that conversion of property is not property damage, it is the taking or deprivation of property; the loss of use of property is different from loss of property in that the loss of use refers to the rental value of similar property that the owner can hire for use during the period when he is deprived of the use of his own property. On the other hand, disappearance of property does result in loss of use of that property by its owner, so the definition of property damage on the CGL form is met and, if the insured is found legally liable for that loss, the CGL form can apply.

The CGL form itself addresses some questions that might arise as to what property damage includes. For example, the CGL form specifically states that "for the purpose of this insurance, electronic data is not tangible property." And, the pollution exclusion on the current CGL form has a paragraph after

its final clauses declaring that the clean up costs part of the exclusion does not apply to liability for damages because of property damage that the insured would have in the absence of any request or demand or order for a clean up. In other words, if the insured is liable for property damage caused by pollution, and the exclusion does not apply for whatever reason, the insurer will not deny coverage for cleaning up the property damage by asserting that the process is simply a clean up cost.

Volunteers and Club Members – Insured under the CGL Forms?

Recently, we have had a number of inquiries regarding the "who is an insured" section of the CGL form where volunteers and members are concerned. We would like to have your considered opinion on the scenarios that are described below.

A local Audubon Society club (the named insured) holds bird watching walks. John, a member, leads the group field trips; Sue, also a member, is a participant in the bird watching field trip led by John. John fails to warn the group that a step is slippery and Sue slips, breaking her ankle. Would Sue be covered by med pay? If she sues, would John be covered by the policy?

A church (the named insured) holds a chili supper in the church basement as a fundraiser. While serving chili to Frank, a member of the church, Jill, a volunteer, spills chili on him, scalding him badly. Would Frank be covered by med pay? If Frank sues, is Jill covered?

Would your answers change if the CGL forms had additional insured endorsements, such as CG 20 02 and CG 20 22, that applies to members?

Indiana Subscriber

Medical payments coverage under the CGL form is for bodily injury caused by an accident on the premises owned by the named insured or because of the operations of the named insured.

Under the first scenario, Sue is covered under the medical payments agreement for medical expenses she incurred for injuries arising out of the Society's operations. If Sue chose to file a lawsuit and name John as a defendant, the CGL policy of the Audubon Society will provide coverage for John under certain circumstances: if he is an employee acting within the scope of his employment; if he is an additional insured on the named insured's policy; or if he is considered a volunteer performing duties related to the conduct of the named insured's business.

Under the second scenario, Frank is covered under the medical payments section of the CGL form. The accident happened on the premises of the named insured and there is no exclusion that would apply to the loss. If Frank sues the church and Jill, the CGL form will, of course, cover the church as the named insured; Jill is an insured due to her status as a volunteer. The current CGL form considers volunteers to be insureds while performing duties related to the conduct of the named insured's business. There may be a question as to whether holding a fundraiser is the business of a church, but since the true business of a church requires the church to have money, and since the CGL form does not specify what it means by using the phrase "conduct of your business", the insured should get the benefit of the doubt in this situation, with coverage applying to its volunteers.

As for the endorsements, CG 20 02 makes club members additional insureds with respect to their liability for the activities they perform on behalf of the named insured, and CG 20 22 does the same for church members and officers.

This means that in the first scenario, John is made an additional insured under the Society's CGL form and so, has coverage if he is sued by Sue, even if he is not an actual employee at the time of the accident; the endorsement has no effect on Sue's ability to collect med pay.

In the second scenario, Frank is still covered for med pay. If Frank sues Jill, she is still covered as an insured due to her status as a volunteer; CG 20 22 does not affect her status as an insured even if she is a member of the church.

BUSINESS AUTO

Auto Coverage for Damaged Driveway?

The insured has a commercial auto policy. The insured was hired by a roofing company to deliver a construction container to a job site. The insured delivered this container to the site as directed. Then, the roofing company official asked the insured to move the container to a different part of the site. While in the process of moving this container, the insured caused damage to the driveway on the site with the truck. As a result, the site owner is filing a property damage claim for the damage to the driveway.

Would this be covered under the insured's auto policy or would coverage be provided by the roofing company since the insured was only following directions?

Missouri Subscriber

The auto policy applies to liability for damages caused by an accident and resulting from the ownership or use of a covered auto. The way you describe this loss, the damage was caused by the use of the insured's truck. Presuming that this was a covered auto, the auto policy of the insured is applicable.

The only reason the roofing company's policy would come into play is if the insured with the auto was listed as an additional insured for some reason on the roofer's policy, or if there was some kind of contractual agreement wherein the roofer had agreed to assume the liability of the trucker for damage done in situations such as this. The fact that the truck driver was following instructions (or requests) from the roofing personnel does not mean the roofing company is responsible for the negligent driving of the vehicle driver.

Auto Policy Versus General Liability Policy Coverage Issue

Our insured was pulling a nonowned trailer. The trailer somehow fell into the mud and was damaged in the amount of over $4,000. The insured has a general liability policy (CGL) and a business auto policy (BAP) with the same carrier, but we are wondering which policy would pay for the loss. What is your opinion?

Indiana Subscriber

Based on the description of the trailer and the loss, neither the BAP nor the CGL form will apply to this loss. This is because both policies have the care, custody, or control exclusion which prevents liability coverage for property damage to property in the care, custody, or control of the insured.

There may be coverage under the auto policy physical damage coverage, but you would have to check to see what the covered auto designation is for that coverage. The physical damage insuring agreement applies to loss to a covered auto or its equipment. So, if the trailer is designated as a covered auto for physical damage coverage, and if the insured has the proper cause of loss coverage, this damage is covered; if not, there is no coverage.

Business Auto Coverage Applicable under Bill of Lading?

Our insured is a fuel jobber/wholesaler who hires common carriers to deliver the fuel to his customers. The common carrier picks up the fuel at a local refinery that has the insured's name on the bill of lading. A very serious accident occurs with several people killed due to the common carrier's negligence. The insured has a business auto policy with symbol 1 (any auto) for the covered auto designation symbol. Will the insured's business auto policy cover him for possible excess exposure when the claimants discover the insured's name on the bill of lading?

Missouri Subscriber

Symbol 1 on the business auto policy designates any auto as a covered auto, and it makes no difference if the auto is owned or not owned by the insured. The symbol also applies to rented cars, leased cars, and borrowed cars. And, the liability insuring agreement applies to all sums that the insured legally must pay due to damages caused by an accident and resulting from the use of a covered auto. So, if the insured is somehow found liable for the injuries here just because of the bill of lading, the use of a covered auto will find coverage for the insured under the auto policy. The coverage is going to be on an excess basis since the covered auto is one that the named insured does not own, but the coverage is present. And, of course, the insured is also entitled to a defense from the insurer.

Collision Coverage Extends to Van Lettering?

Our insured has a van and a business auto policy with collision coverage for the van. If he has an accident and totals the van, we have no problem with paying the actual cash value for the van itself, but a question has arisen about the lettering on the van. Would we owe for the special lettering on the van that the insured says identifies his business?

One side says that the van's actual cash value is the same regardless of the lettering, or that the lettering, in fact, has diminished the value of the van because someone buying the van would have to repaint the vehicle. On the other hand, some say we owe at least a depreciated amount for the lettering as it was part of the vehicle and the insured will have to replace the lettering on a new van.

What is your opinion? And if the lettering should be paid for, how is it included in the payment calculations?

Ohio Subscriber

The lettering on the van may be seen as diminishing the value for someone who did not own the van, but for the insured who did own it and who did insure it, the van's lettering did not diminish the value. It perhaps even increased the value of the van by helping the insured's his business, albeit indirectly, by getting his business name out there before the public.

And, the lettering is part of the van since it was made a physical part of the van. It is not excluded by the policy language as are other items. If the insurer had wanted to exclude the lettering, it would have been easy to add the lettering to the excluded items like electronic equipment or radar detectors, but this was not done. So, the insured is entitled to the reasonable assumption that the lettering was not meant to be excluded.

The insured also has to be put back into the same position he was in prior to the loss. He no doubt paid for the lettering, making the lettering a value added, and made it part of his van. So, if the lettering is not paid for, the insured is losing value. That would violate the principle of indemnity.

Finally, consider if this was only a partial loss to the side of the van that has the lettering. The policy would pay for the cost of repair with like kind and quality and that would include the lettering. A total loss should not be handled differently in that the lettering would be considered part of the loss.

Presuming then that the lettering is covered for loss, the insured can be consulted as to how much he paid for the lettering. That amount less depreciation would be paid since the loss for a covered auto is paid on an ACV basis with an adjustment

made for depreciation and physical condition. But, if there is a disagreement on the amount of loss, the appraisal clause on the auto policy does allow for either the insured or the insurer to demand an appraisal of the loss.

Coverage Territory Dispute under BAP

We would like your opinion about the following issue.

We have an insured that purchased a vehicle in California. The vehicle was being driven to Canada to an employee who is domiciled in Canada; ultimately, the vehicle would have been domiciled in Canada. In route, however, before delivery of the vehicle was made to the employee, the vehicle was involved in an accident in Canada. The insurer is denying coverage for the claim on the basis that the vehicle was domiciled Canada and the BAP does not cover such vehicles. Is this correct?

California Subscriber

The BAP covers accidents and losses that occur within the coverage territory and the coverage territory is defined as the United States, its territories and possessions, Puerto Rico, and Canada (and anywhere in the world under certain circumstances). And, the BAP also covers loss to or accidents involving a covered auto while being transported between any of these places. The accident in Canada is covered.

Whether the car was to be domiciled in Canada is mainly a rating issue and/or a policy type issue since Canada has its own insurance system that is different from the U.S. version. Perhaps the insurer is thinking about out of state coverage extensions or liability determination lawsuits, but those are items concerned with the liability of the insured for bodily injury or property damage. But, if this is just a physical damage claim, and if the car was a covered auto at the time of the accident and the insured has the proper cause of loss coverage (probably collision coverage based on your description of the loss), this accident will be covered.

Diminished Value

A new car was stolen from our insured auto dealer's lot. The vehicle was driven to another state and abandoned. The police recovered the car and returned it to the insured, but the car had about 3,000 miles put on it by the thieves. There was no physical damage to the car but the insured says the car cannot be sold as "new" because of the mileage, so he has suffered a loss. The insurer sees this as an indirect loss, one of diminished value, and so not covered by the auto policy. What is your opinion? Further, how would this be handled if the auto policy were a personal auto policy?

New York Subscriber

It is our opinion that the vehicle did not suffer a "loss" as defined on the business auto policy. The physical damage section of the auto policy applies to direct and accidental loss or damage to the covered auto. Direct loss is just that—a direct physical loss to the auto. A loss in value, in that the car cannot be sold as new, is diminution in value and that is not physical damage. The majority of courts throughout the country that have heard the issue say that diminution in value is not physical damage to the covered property. Moreover, the current business auto policy has an exclusion that prevents paying for a claim for diminution in value. The policy defines diminution in value as the actual or perceived loss in market value or resale value which results from a direct or accidental loss. That describes the situation in which the insured finds himself and so, the auto policy will not cover this claim.

As for the personal auto policy (PAP), the opinion is the same. It is true that the current personal auto policy does not have a diminution in value exclusion like the business auto policy does; however, the physical damage coverage agreement on the PAP applies to "direct and accidental loss to the covered auto" and that language does not include an indirect loss such as diminution in value. There is an endorsement (PP 13 01 12 99) that revises the physical damage section of the PAP by declaring that the insurer will not pay for loss to the covered auto due to diminution in value, but this endorsement is not yet approved in all jurisdictions.

Direct and Accidental Loss Discussed

A claim has been presented for the discoloration and cloudiness of the left and right plastic headlamp lenses on the insured's covered auto. The lenses are not cracked or broken. The repair shop reported that the discoloration/cloudiness is on the exterior of the lenses and results from environmental issues over time such as the effects of sunlight and/or acid rain. The headlamps function as they are supposed to, so we do not see any coverage for this claim. What do you think?

Maine Subscriber

The business auto policy defines a loss as direct and accidental loss or damage. This means actual physical damage to the covered auto caused by an accident. Based on the repair shop report, there was no damage by accident in this instance; this was simply something that happened naturally over time. But, even if this were deemed to be a loss as defined, the wear and tear exclusion would apply since that exclusion is meant to prevent coverage for loss or damage that an auto suffers naturally due to the stress and strain (or wear and tear) put on a car by its daily use.

Equipment Physical Damage Coverage under the BAP

Our insured has a snow plow for the front of his vehicle. Pieces of the snow plow had been disconnected from the insured vehicle and were sitting on the ground outside of the insured's business. Someone stole the equipment.

My question is, are the pieces of the plow that were stolen covered under the auto physical damage portion of the policy? My thought is that the pieces should be covered since they have no use unless they are connected to the snow plow on the front of the vehicle. The parts that were stolen are a lift frame, lights and an E60 unit. What is your opinion?

Minnesota Subscriber

The physical damage coverage under the business auto policy is for a covered auto or its equipment. There is no requirement under the terms of the policy that the equipment be in or on the covered auto at the time of loss. There is no exclusion that would apply in this instance as you describe it. So, if the equipment had no use other than for the covered auto's plow, it is covered under the terms of the auto policy, as long as the insured had the appropriate cause of loss coverage.

Explosives Transported by Insured and BAP Coverage

We insured a trucker with an auto liability policy. Endorsement CA 23 01 12 93, explosives, is attached to the policy. One of our producers raised the question as to how the explosive exclusion on this endorsement would apply to any hazardous materials an insured might haul. For example, if the insured were to haul some type of flammable gas, chemical, or liquid that required a HAZMAT placard, would the exclusion come into play?

Georgia Subscriber

CA 23 01 does not define the word "explosive", so you would have to check the dictionary to see what that term includes. But, the standard dictionary defines an explosive as a substance that bursts forth with sudden violence and noise from internal energy. That certainly fits flammable gas or chemicals or liquids that require a HAZMAT sticker.

CA 23 01 is a rather extensive exclusion. It affects the business auto policy, the motor carrier and the truckers coverage forms. The main purpose behind the exclusion, based on the coverage forms that it modifies, is to prevent any coverage for bodily injury or property damage that may occur while the named insured is transporting any explosives and the explosives explode during this transit.

But the way it is written, the exclusion prevents coverage while in transit, and also prevents coverage if the named insured makes or sells the explosives. So, no matter when the explosives explode, in transit or not, if the named insured makes or sells them, this endorsement precludes any coverage for the named insured. And, the wording can also be viewed as preventing coverage even if after a transport has been completed. As long as the insured transported the explosives, it can be said that the explosives were those that the insured had transported, so the exclusion applies.

The only way the endorsement would not be effective, or at least would be open to question, would be if the named insured did not make or sell the explosives and did not directly transport the explosives, but contracted with another carrier to do so. For example, if the maker of the explosives came to the named insured and contracted to transport the explosives, and the insured then contracted with another carrier to do the actual transportation, and an explosion occurred, a case could be made that the exclusion did not apply because the named insured did not actually transport the explosives. This would boil down to a legal issue, as to whether the insured did or did not transport the explosives, albeit vicariously. This is a legal question that we cannot answer. You may want to consult with an attorney in your area to see what the legal view is on this point.

Fire Department Service Fee Covered by Auto Policy?

Some municipalities send out the fire department to an auto accident scene just in case the department is needed. There may be a law or statute requiring the fire department to then send a bill for services to the insured. Would the auto policy pay this bill even if the insured was not at fault? For an accident involving only the insured's car?

Kentucky Subscriber

There is generally no coverage under the business auto policy for fire department fees.

The liability coverage under the auto policy is for liability for bodily injury or property damage, both defined terms on the policy. Neither definition includes a fee or charge for fire department services. And, the supplementary payments

section of the policy does not include any such fee. Now, if the insured is involved in an at-fault accident and some bodily injury or property damage occurs, and the damages for which the insured becomes liable include a fire department service fee, then that will be paid under the terms of the auto policy. For example, if the insured crashes into someone and injures the other driver and the fire department has to rush to the accident scene to rescue or treat the injured person, and a department service fee is included in the sums that the insured becomes legally obligated to pay, then the liability coverage section of the auto policy will respond.

There would not be any coverage for fire department service fees under the physical damage section of the auto policy because that coverage is just for physical damage to the covered auto. Fire department service fees are not part of such coverage.

Freezing Exclusion Affects Coverage for Damage to Scheduled Auto?

Our insured had his scheduled auto garaged outside, open to the elements. Cracks developed in the fiberglass and the repair facility said that the cracks were probably started as a result of hail or falling branches. The cracks resulted in a seal failure ultimately causing extensive water and freeze damage to the fiberglass and the underlying wood panel.

The freezing exclusion on the auto policy applies to loss caused by or resulting from freezing and we are unsure how to interpret the exclusion in relation to this loss. Please comment.

Connecticut Subscriber

The freezing exclusion in the business auto policy reads as follows: we will not pay for loss caused by or resulting from freezing unless caused by other loss that is covered. So, if the repair facility is correct, the freezing loss was caused by an other loss, that is, hail or falling branches. This means that the loss is a covered loss as long as the insured had the appropriate coverage, comprehensive coverage.

The freezing exclusion will not apply.

Hired Auto Coverage Available When Employee Rents Auto?

The insured has a business auto policy (BAP) with symbol 8, hired autos only, under the liability coverage section. The insured employs several traveling salesmen and if an employee rents a car on a business trip, we are wondering about coverage for the insured and the employee. If the employee, while driving a rented car on the business of the named insured, causes an accident and a claim is made against the insured and the employee, will the BAP provide coverage for them?

Ohio Subscriber

Symbol 8 describes covered autos as only those autos that the named insured leases, hires, or borrows. If the car is rented in the name of the named insured, then there is liability coverage for the named insured and the employee as someone using the rented car with permission. If the car is rented in the name of the employee, there can be a problem with coverage.

Since symbol 8 describes an auto that the named insured (you) hires or rents as a covered auto, it follows that an auto rented by the employee, who is not the named insured, is not a covered auto. And, since the liability insuring agreement is for the use of a covered auto, the absence of such a vehicle gives grounds for the insurer to deny coverage should an accident occur with the rented car.

What the insured may want to consider is using endorsement CA 20 54 10 01, employee hired autos. This endorsement makes an employee an insured while operating an auto hired or rented under a contract or agreement in that employee's name, with the permission of the named insured, while performing duties related to the conduct of the business of the named insured. As for coverage for the named insured, the endorsement does not address the status of the named insured, so there are other options for the named insured.

The named insured can either change the covered auto designation to symbol 1, any auto, or add symbol 9, nonowned autos, which are autos that the named insured does not own, lease, hire, rent or borrow that are used in the named insured's business. This would make the car rented by the employee a covered auto for the liability coverage purposes of the named insured.

Or, the named insured can rely on paragraph c. of the who is an insured provisions in the BAP. This paragraph considers as an insured anyone liable for the conduct of an insured, and since the employee is an insured through the use of CA 20 54 and the named insured, as the employer, is liable for the conduct of the employee/insured, paragraph c. would provide liability coverage for the named insured.

Or, the named insured can rely on court rulings that the word "you" includes both the named insured employer and the employee since a named insured that is a corporation or some other business cannot act except through employees. This way, any liability coverage provided for "you" will apply to both the named insured and the employee.

There are ways to assure that both the named insured/employer and the employee are covered for liability claims arising from the use of a rented car. Which way is most acceptable is, of course, up to the named insured, taking into consideration his own business situation.

Insured Contract and Specifically Described Auto Coverage

Our insured has a business auto policy with symbol 7 (specifically described auto) for liability coverage. The insured rented a car recently and was involved in an accident, resulting in a liability claim. The rental contract had a hold harmless and indemnity agreement in favor of the rental company.

The use of symbol 7 would prevent coverage being extended due to the use of a rented car, but we are wondering about the rental agreement and contractual liability. The contractual exclusion on the auto policy excludes liability assumed under any contract except for liability assumed in an insured contract. The car rental agreement was an insured contract by definition, so it appears that there may be coverage based on an insured contract. On the other hand, there is no liability coverage arising out of the use of a covered auto since the rented car was not a symbol 7 auto. Does the contractual exclusion and insured contract exception even come into play?

Ohio Subscriber

We don't see any coverage here. The auto liability coverage is for bodily injury or property damage caused by an accident and resulting from the use or ownership of a covered auto. The key phrase is "covered auto". By the use of symbol 7, the insured did not make the rented car a covered auto. So, the insuring agreement terms have not been met.

The insuring agreement has to be met first and then, the exclusions and conditions and definitions have to be examined to see how or if the insuring agreement coverage is affected. The contractual exclusion's exception would have applied if the insuring agreement was applicable, but since that is not the case, the contractual exclusion language does not even come into play. The insured made a mistake in his covered auto designation choice and the auto policy will not make up for that mistake.

You did not mention coverage for the damage done to the rented car. The care, custody or control exclusion would prevent liability coverage for that damage regardless of the presence of an insured contract. And, in fact, the definition of an insured contract on the auto policy states that a contract that obligates the insured to pay for property damage to any auto rented or leased by the insured is not considered an insured contract.

Motor Carrier Coverage for Nonowned Vehicle

Under the terms of the motor carrier coverage form, CA 00 20 03 06, does the policy provide primary or excess coverage to the named insured for a nonowned vehicle? Does it provide primary coverage to a sub-hauler who uses his own equipment? And, if there is a sub-haul agreement, would the nonowned unit be considered as being used in the named insured's business?

North Carolina Subscriber

As a general rule, coverage for an auto that the named insured does not own is excess and coverage for an owned auto is primary. But, the motor carrier coverage form has exceptions to note.

If the named insured hires or borrows another's vehicle, the coverage is primary if a written agreement between the named insured (as lessee) and the other party (as lessor) does not require the lessor to hold the named insured harmless. This is so only while the covered auto is used exclusively in the business of the named insured as a motor carrier for hire.

The coverage is excess over any other collectible insurance if a written agreement between the other party and the named insured requires the other party to hold the named insured harmless.

If the named insured has another party hire or borrow a vehicle owned by the named insured, the coverage is primary if the written agreement between the named insured (lessor) and the other party requires the named insured to hold that other party harmless. And, the coverage is excess over any other collectible insurance if the agreement does not require the named insured to hold the other party (lessee) harmless.

Any trailer interchange coverage is primary for any covered auto. Trailer interchange coverage applies to all sums the insured must legally pay as damages because of a loss to a trailer that the named insured does not own. This is similar to physical damage coverage but based on the legal liability of the named insured, and applies when the named insured uses the trailer of another in his business; this is a routinely used business practice in the motor carrier business.

Finally, the coverage under CA 00 20 is primary for the named insured for any liability assumed under an insured contract, a defined term on the policy.

So basically, each instance has to be judged on the factual situation to see whether the coverage provided by CA 00 20 is primary or excess.

Pollution Attributed to Vandalism

We recently had a claim where a covered auto (a fuel tanker-trailer) was damaged by vandals when they ran a piece of mobile equipment into the tanker. A damaged valve allowed several thousand gallons of diesel fuel to spill, which had to be cleaned up.

ISO's commercial auto policy CA 00 01 (03 06 edition) section II states the company will pay "covered pollution cost or expense" (a defined term) under certain circumstances. Covered pollution cost or expense does not include any cost or expense arising out of the release or escape of pollutants being stored or transported in or upon a covered auto; and, in fact, the pollution exclusion on the auto policy also applies to such an incident. However, an exception to the exclusionary language states there is coverage for "pollutants" needed for the normal or mechanical functioning of the covered auto, if the "pollutants" are released directly from an auto part designed by its manufacturer to hold or store such "pollutants."

It is this exception that we think gives the potential for coverage. The common person would think the normal mechanical function of the tanker is to store fuel, and it is specifically designed by its manufacturer to hold, store, and dispose of such fuel.

Iowa Subscriber

The operative word that prevents the exception to the pollution exclusion and the covered pollution cost or expense coverage of the business auto policy from applying to the kind of loss you describe is, we believe, "normal." The exception language refers to pollutants "that are needed for or result from the normal electrical, hydraulic, or mechanical functioning of the covered auto or its parts." What was released in this instance was fuel that was being stored in the tanker, and that has nothing to do with the normal electrical or hydraulic or mechanical functioning of the covered auto. What the exception refers to is something like the oil or gasoline that allows the auto to function. So, for example, if the vandals had damaged the crank case or the fuel tank of the auto and oil or gas had leaked out, the damage caused by that pollution spill would be covered by the auto policy. That is not what happened in this instance. The leakage that occurs after the valve on the storage tank has been damaged by vandalism does not equate with the normal mechanical functioning of the tanker.

Pollution Cleanup Costs Covered by BAP?

Our insured is a long haul trucker insured under the business auto policy (BAP). He has a company specific endorsement that provides broadened coverage for pollution liability claims. In this instance, the insured was in possession of a nonowned refrigerated trailer and had completed a delivery. Before returning the trailer to its owner, the insured disconnected the trailer for the weekend. Over the weekend, the refrigeration unit on the trailer leaked diesel fuel, possibly due to poor maintenance by the trailer owner. Would the pollution clean up be covered by our insured's auto policy?

Massachusetts Subscriber

There are several things to be considered in this coverage question.

First, the insured has to be liable for the leak so that he legally has to pay for the cleanup. We cannot answer questions about legal liability so you may want to check with an attorney in your area to see if the insured is liable for the clean up costs based on the circumstances of his using a nonowned trailer that possibly was in need of repair work.

Second, the auto policy will pay for bodily injury or property due to a pollution leak or spill if the pollutants are fuels or fluids or lubricants needed for the normal electrical or mechanical functioning of the covered auto or its parts, and if the pollutants escape from a part designed by its manufacturer to hold such pollutants. In this instance, diesel fuel from the refrigeration unit would fit into the exception to the pollution exclusion, except for the question of whether the nonowned trailer is a covered auto. The BAP does consider trailers not owned by the named insured to be covered autos for liability purposes, but only while attached to power units owned by the named insured. That is not the case here. Furthermore, there has to be either bodily injury or property damage caused by the accident. So, there has to be some property damage here and not just a cleanup charge.

The auto policy does provide coverage for a covered pollution cost or expense as defined on the policy, but here again, there has to be some bodily injury or property damage due to the auto accident before a covered pollution cost or expense is paid.

Third, if the insured is legally liable for the spill and there is some property damage, you have to check the wording on the company specific endorsement

75

to see how it modifies the standard pollution exclusion. There is an ISO endorsement, CA 99 55 03 06, that provides broadened coverage for pollution liability claims and that may act as a guideline for interpreting your endorsement (even though the ISO form applies to the garage coverage form).

CA 99 55 changes the pollution exclusion (for covered autos) on the coverage form so that paragraph a., pertaining to a leak of pollutants contained in any property in the course of transit by the insured, applies only to liability assumed under a contract or agreement. The way you describe the situation here, the trailer can be considered to still be in the course of transit since it was not yet returned to the owner at the time of the leak. So, paragraph a. of the pollution exclusion would not apply to a claim for bodily injury or property damage in this instance. CA 99 55 also revises the definition of covered pollution cost or expense to include the type of claim that you describe, a leak of pollutants from property in the course of transit by the insured.

In summary, the insured can have coverage for this leak of pollutants, but he has to be liable for the spill, there has to be some property damage involved and not just cleanup expenses, and the wording on the insured's endorsement has to be like the wording on CA 99 55.

Tire Damage Covered under Auto Policy?

We insure a truck under a commercial auto policy. A tire blew out causing substantial damage to the surrounding fenders, but there was no collision involved. The total amount of the claim is in excess of $13,000. The insurer is denying coverage for the damage to the tires and the rest of the truck. The basis for the denial is the exclusion for loss caused by or resulting from blowouts, punctures, or other road damage to tires.

I understand the exclusion not providing coverage for the tires, but I find it hard to believe that the intent is to exclude subsequent body damage to the rest of the vehicle. What is your opinion?

Indiana Subscriber

The wording of the tire damage exclusion on the auto policy is not very clear. It is convoluted and can be very confusing to the insured. It is true that the phrase "loss caused by or resulting from …" can be seen as excluding a loss that results from a blowout or puncture or other tire damage. But, we are of the opinion that the exclusion does not apply to the vehicle damage in this instance.

Exclusions are meant to be read narrowly and any reasonable ambiguity has to be interpreted in favor of the insured. In this vein, this exclusion can be interpreted this way: the insurer will not pay for loss caused by blowouts, punctures, or other road damage TO TIRES. In other words, the auto policy is not going to pay to cover normal road damage to tires, period. Damage to tires caused by fire or a collision or some other covered cause of loss is covered, but normal everyday road conditions damage to tires is not covered.

This is a reasonable interpretation of the exclusion. In our opinion, to extend that exclusion beyond road damage to tires is not the intent. The exclusion is ambiguous and the intended scope of the exclusion does not go beyond normal road damage to tires; the damage to the fenders in this case is not excluded by the tire damage exclusion.

Trailer Stolen from Business Premises Covered by Auto Policy?

Our insured has a businessowners policy (BOP) and a business auto policy (BAP). The insured's trailer was stolen from the business premises while unattached to any vehicle. In this area, the trailer is required to be registered and licensed.

The BOP excludes coverage for the loss of vehicles that are required to be registered and licensed. The BAP uses symbol 7 (specifically described autos) as the covered auto designation symbol, and the trailer was not listed in the policy's schedule as required by the use of symbol 7.

Based on this information, we do not think that the loss of the trailer is covered by either policy. What is your opinion?

South Carolina Subscriber

We agree with you that the BOP will not offer coverage for the theft of the trailer; it was clearly excluded. But, when it comes to the BAP, coverage will depend on the symbol used for physical damage coverage.

The BAP applies to loss to a covered auto and an auto includes a trailer by definition. The trailer does not have to be attached to any other vehicle for the purpose of physical damage coverage; that is a requirement for liability coverage if the trailer is not owned by the named insured. What is required for physical damage coverage is a covered loss to a covered auto.

So, theft coverage here depends on the symbol used for physical damage coverage. For example, if the insured has symbol 1, any auto, for his physical damage coverage, that would apply to the theft of the trailer as a covered auto. If the insured has symbol 7 for physical damage coverage and the trailer is not specifically described, then we would agree with you about the lack of coverage under the BAP. It basically depends on what symbol was used for the physical damage coverage and, of course, if the insured had the comprehensive or specified causes of loss coverage, both of which include loss due to theft.

Care, Custody, or Control Exclusion and Truck Damage

 *We insure a company that has symbol 1, any auto, on its business auto policy (BAP). This insured hired two trucks with drivers. We covered both the trucks and the owner operators for liability purposes on our insured's BAP. The insured does not carry physical damage coverage, however.*

One of the trucks ran into the second truck. Would our insured's liability coverage apply to the physical damage to the second truck, or does the care, custody, or control exclusion apply?

Kansas Subscriber

Liability coverage would be available for your insured for the damage to the second truck if he is found to be liable for the damage.

The care, custody, or control exclusion applies to the insured who has custody and control of the property that is damaged. In this case, the truck that was damaged (truck #2) was not in the custody of your insured. If the insurance company wanted the exclusion to apply more broadly, it could have chosen to exclude coverage for property in the care, custody, or control of "an" or "any" insured. But that is not how the exclusion reads. The word used is "the", and that makes the exclusion pertinent only to that particular insured who has care, custody, or control of the property at the time the property is damaged.

As for the driver of the truck that caused the damage, he would not usually be considered an insured for this accident. The who is an insured clauses in the business auto policy declare that the owner of the auto that is hired or borrowed by the named insured is not considered to be an insured under the named insured's policy. But apparently your policy contradicts this standard wording and makes the driver/owner/operator an insured. If that is so, the care, custody, or control exclusion will not apply to the first truck driver either because he did not have care, custody, or control of the property that was damaged, that is, the second truck.

So, the auto policy will provide coverage for both the insureds in this instance should a claim be made against them for the damage to the second truck. The care, custody, or control exclusion is not applicable to the liability claim.

Wear and Tear Exclusion

An insured went away for the weekend and left his truck with the battery charging for three days at home. When he returned, the battery had over-charged and acid had mixed with the gasoline, changing into sulfuric acid. The fumes contaminated the entire vehicle. The truck was unusable because the sulfuric acid caused skin irritation when a person got close to the truck. Additionally, all the metal on the truck turned green.

Our question is whether the business auto policy's exclusion of damage caused by wear and tear, mechanical breakdown, and electrical failure would apply?

Illinois Subscriber

Even though it was probably the normal wear and tear of the battery that caused it to become uncharged and caused it to fail to hold a charge, this wear and tear was not the direct cause of the loss. The direct cause of the loss was putting more electricity into the battery than it could hold.

The mechanical breakdown exclusion is not applicable simply because nothing mechanical really broke down.

And, the creation of sulfuric acid fumes from acid overflowing the battery is not the electrical breakdown referred to in the exclusion. That portion of the exclusion refers to damage caused by wire connections separating or by the friction of wires rubbing, leading to broken or short circuits.

This loss was not caused by any of these exclusions. The loss was caused by the sulfuric acid fumes which were caused by an electrical overcharge (not an electrical breakdown).

GARAGE

Appraisal for Physical Damage Loss Issue

The insured's garage policy contains a loss condition as follows: if you and we disagree on the amount of loss, either may demand an appraisal of the loss. In this event, each party will select a competent appraiser. The two appraisers will select a competent and impartial umpire. The appraisers will state separately the actual cash value and amount of loss. If they fail to agree, they will submit their differences to the umpire. A decision agreed to by any two will be binding.

Our insured recently suffered a hail loss to multiple vehicles. We hired an independent appraiser who wrote estimates using paintless dent repair. The insured secured another independent appraiser who wrote estimates using the conventional repair method. Of course, the two estimates of loss were different and the dispute went to the chosen umpire. The umpire advised that the insured's estimate was too low, but he did not accept our estimate either.

The question is: does the appraisal condition require the umpire to simply agree with one of the estimates, or does the condition allow the umpire to write his own estimate?

Georgia Subscriber

The appraisal clause gives the umpire authority to either agree with the separate appraisers or to come up with an opinion of his own. There is no restriction in the clause as to the duties of the umpire. He only need be competent and impartial. The key point in the clause is that two of the three parties must agree on the appraisal for it to be binding on the insured and the insurer. As examples: if the umpire agrees with the insurer's appraisal, they are the two agreeing parties called for in the clause; if the insured's appraiser agrees with an appraisal that the umpire comes up with, they are the two agreeing parties.

So long as the appraisal clause does not specifically require the umpire to limit his opinion to one or the other of the two competing appraisals, he is free to come up with his own if he chooses, and then try to get one or the other of the parties to agree with him.

Care, Custody, or Control Exclusion Issue

Does the care, custody, or control exclusion in the garage policy apply to a building that the insured rents? Our insured rents a building in which he operates his garage repair service. An employee ran a customer's car into the building and caused extensive damage to both the building and the car. Is the building excluded from the liability coverage the insured has under his policy? I have not read the lease, so I don't know what that says about such an occurrence.

Michigan Subscriber

The care, custody, or control exclusion on the garage form applies to property damage to property in the insured's care, custody, or control. This is not limited to personal property, so the exclusion does apply to real property over which the insured has custody or control, like this building. But furthermore, that same exclusion on the garage form excludes coverage for property damage to property rented or occupied by the insured. Either way, the insured does not have liability coverage under his garage policy for the damage done to the building.

You did not ask about coverage for the damage to the customer's car, so we presume that the insured has garagekeepers coverage and that will take care of the damage done to the car.

Finally, for informational purposes, you should get a copy of the lease and peruse it just to be sure what your insured is liable for due to the damage done to the building.

Direct Primary Coverage Option under GKLL

Our insured has garagekeepers coverage on a direct primary coverage option. A customer's auto was in the insured's garage for repairs and was vandalized. The customer turned in a claim to his own insurer and that was paid, minus the deductible. That insurer then subrogated against our insured based on the insured being liable for the damage. But, the auto was damaged by vandals and we do not believe that our insured is liable.

Since the customer already went through his own insurance policy for payment for the damage and since our insured is not liable for the damage, should our policy pay anything? This is our question, especially since subrogation is based on liability and our insured is not liable. What are your thoughts?

Colorado Subscriber

We cannot address the question of liability since that is a legal issue. That would have to be settled in the courtroom in your area in accordance with your state laws.

However, when it comes to the issue of insurance coverage, the direct primary coverage option under garagekeepers makes the question of liability irrelevant. Under the direct primary option, garagekeepers coverage is changed to apply without regard to the legal liability of the named insured or any other insured for a loss to a customer's car; this coverage is on a primary basis. This coverage is basically goodwill coverage for the insured since it is meant to pay for damage to a customer's car that happens when the car is in the care of the insured, it is meant to pay upfront with little or no problems so that the customer can have his auto repaired without going through any legal battles over who is responsible for the damage.

And, since the direct primary coverage option is primary insurance, that has to be compared with the primary insurance coverage that the customer has under his own auto policy. If two policies promise primary coverage, property adjusting traditions and, more often than not, policy language call for the two policies to prorate the loss payment. The garage policy does call for pro-rata payments if the coverage forms are on the same basis, either excess or primary. You may want to see if the customer's auto policy does this too.

It would have been easier for everyone if the customer had let your insured handle the loss based on the direct primary coverage option. However, since that is not the situation, the loss payment for the damage to the car should be split between the customer's insurance policy and the GKLL coverage. If the customer's insurer is subrogating for this pro-rata payment, that is not necessary since the direct primary coverage option requires such a payment; if the insurer is subrogating for the entire payment, that is a lawsuit based on the legal liability of the insured and that, as noted above, is not something we can address.

False Pretense Coverage for Auto Dealership

Our insured is an auto dealership and he has false pretense coverage on his garage form. The insured suffered a loss recently when he sold a car to someone under false pretenses. The car was recovered undamaged, but the insured is making a claim for numerous costs and expenses associated with the sale of the vehicle, along with a diminished value due to the mileage put on the car by the former driver. The insured is looking for coverage for the following items: registration and other miscellaneous fees; preparation fees; upfront money; lost sales commission; and lost profit.

It is our opinion that under the false pretense coverage, we may owe the actual reduction in the value of the car since it can no longer be sold as a new car, but we do not owe for the fees, commissions, or other amounts claimed by the insured. What is your opinion?

Tennessee Subscriber

False pretense coverage applies to loss to a covered auto, with loss being a defined term. You have to look at the garage coverage form for the definition since the false pretense endorsement modifies the garage form, and there is no separate definition of "loss" on the endorsement.

Loss is defined as direct and accidental loss or damage. Direct and accidental loss or damage means the actual direct physical damage done to a covered auto. The fees and expenses and diminution in value (excluded by a specific exclusion on the garage form) that the insured is claiming are not direct losses; they are consequential losses, indirect losses, and economic losses. The false pretense coverage does not apply to such items.

Garage Coverage for False Pretense Claims

We have some questions about the false pretense coverage that can be attached to a garage policy.

A customer comes into the insured's shop and wants to but a motorcycle. The customer provides a drivers license and a credit card for proof of identity. A credit application is completed and forwarded to the finance company. The application is approved and the sale made. Some time later, the customer defaults and by virtue of the contractual indemnity provisions in the contract between the finance company and our insured, the finance company can charge back the insured for the amount defaulted on. Would the chargeback payments be covered by the false pretense coverage?

In this same scenario, would it make a difference if the customer used false identification?

If the customer had paid for the motorcycle with a check that bounced due to, for example the account being closed or not having sufficient funds to cover the check, how would the false pretense coverage respond?

Texas Subscriber

False pretense coverage applies when the insured has a loss to a covered auto by voluntarily parting with the vehicle by trick or under false pretense. If the buyer in this instance defaulted on the contract between the finance company and him, this does not necessarily mean that there were false pretenses involved in the sale between your insured and the customer. The false pretense coverage will not pay the finance company back for its finances. The contract between the insured and company is just that, an agreement between those two parties, and it has nothing to do with the false pretense coverage.

If the customer used a false ID to get the vehicle that would be a false pretense loss and the endorsement would pay for the loss of the vehicle. This does not mean paying the finance company its lost money. The insured probably would have to reimburse the finance company on his own because of the contract between them, but that is not the subject of the false pretense coverage; the false pretense coverage is for the insured only.

There is an exclusion on the false pretense endorsement pertaining to a loss in which for any reason a bank or any other drawee fails to pay. That would apply in your last scenario since the bank, for whatever reason, would not pay the money due to the insured for the vehicle.

Garage Operations Incidental to Garage Business at Issue

The definition of garage operations on the garage policy includes all operations necessary or incidental to a garage business. But, the definition does not elaborate on what an incidental operation is. Can you clarify this item?

New Hampshire Subscriber

The answer is, not to any great degree. But as usual with any insurance policy, if a term or phrase is ambiguous or not defined in the policy, the insured is entitled to any reasonable doubt settled in his favor.

One might check the dictionary to see how incidental is defined, but that definition is not very useful either since it only refers to some minor event or something that is subordinate to something else of greater importance. Courts have been reluctant generally to extend the interpretation of the word "incidental" to include anything and everything that may occur on the premises of a garage risk, but have instead made their decisions on a case by case basis, with the facts of the operations being given great weight. For example, car rental operations have been held as incidental operations to a garage business. The selling of shotgun shells at a service station was held not to be incidental operations.

In summary, there is no concrete, definitive answer to the question of what an incidental operation is when it comes to garage operations. Insureds and insurers need to scrutinize all operations and come to an agreement on what is

to be included as incidental operations before the garage coverage is written, and certainly before any loss involving those incidental operations arises.

Garagekeepers Coverage Pays for Profit Charge?

Our insured has damaged a customer's car while servicing the vehicle. There is no dispute about coverage the damage claim. The issue is the repair charge. Our insured wants to do the repair work himself and we are not sure if he is entitled to the profit on parts and labor just as any other repair shop would be. Some in our office want to eliminate any such payment, but others say there is nothing in the policy language to allow such action. What is your opinion?

Ohio Subscriber

Garagekeepers coverage is a liability coverage. The insuring agreement calls for the policy to pay all sums that the insured legally must pay as damages. The coverage does allow for a deductible, but, as you point out, there is no provision for eliminating profit from the legal liability charge.

Therefore, unless there is a court ruling or state law pertaining to the subject of the insured's profiting for his work, some common sense would be in order. Would those who deny that profit should be included in the payment prefer to have the repair work done by someone other than the insured? There would be no issue about eliminating the profit in that instance, so why should the issue arise just because the insured wants to do the work? Besides, the insured is investing his time and labor in the repair work, and the parts used by him are not being given to him by the parts manufacturers for free, so equity demands that the insured receive compensation for these costs.

Another point to consider is the fact that if an insurance policy is ambiguous in its language, or, as in this case, lacking any clarity at all, the insured is entitled to the benefit of any reasonable doubt. The insured should be paid for his profit charge in this claim.

Garagekeepers Coverage for a Stolen Auto

Our insured is covered by a garagekeepers policy. He was conducting a state mandated inspection on a car, performing an emissions test for which the engine had to be running. At this point an unknown person jumped into the vehicle and stole it. The insurance company is denying coverage because the adjuster does not feel that our insured is legally liable. The adjuster stated "what could the insured have done to prevent the theft?"

What is your opinion of this coverage question?

Pennsylvania Subscriber

Garagekeepers legal liability coverage is based on the insured's being legally liable for loss to a customer's auto. The adjuster is wrong to assume that the insured is not legally liable in this case. Whether there is legal liability is a question of law that should be settled in a court, and unless the adjuster is an attorney familiar with the law in Pennsylvania, he should not be making legal interpretations. We likewise cannot answer questions about legal liability, but if it is established that the insured was legally liable for the loss of the customer's car, we can review the garagekeepers insurance coverage to see if that coverage would apply to this claim.

The loss of this car was direct and accidental (certainly from the viewpoint of the insured). Since it was a theft, the insured had to have comprehensive coverage or specified causes of loss coverage under his garagekeepers form for the insurance to apply. There is no exclusion that would apply since the theft exclusion under the garagekeepers coverage applies to loss due to theft or conversion caused by the named insured or his employees. That is not the case here.

As for what the insured could have done to prevent the theft, that is not a relevant point. The insured had the car in his care at the time of loss. The garagekeepers insuring agreement and the provisions in that coverage simply require the loss of the customer's auto to occur while the car is in the care of the insured; they do not say anything about coverage depending on whether the insured could or could not have prevented a theft.

Garagekeepers Coverage on a Direct Excess Basis

We have a question dealing with garagekeepers legal liability coverage written on a direct excess basis. Does the direct excess coverage void liability coverage altogether, or is the direct excess coverage an additional coverage that does not affect the insurer's obligation to pay when the insured is legally liable?

The case in point occurred when the insured's negligence started a fire in a customer's vehicle. Since the customer had comprehensive coverage, the customer's carrier paid for the damage; and, since the insured was legally liable, the customer's carrier subrogated against the insured. The insured's carrier denied coverage, saying the direct excess option removed liability coverage for the insured. The insured contends that he has paid

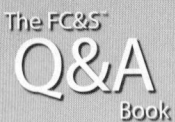

extra premium for the direct excess option and that his insurer should pay for this claim regardless of that option.

Pennsylvania Subscriber

We agree with your insured that he has not lost his legal liability coverage. Garagekeepers coverage is based on the legal liability of the insured. Under the direct excess option, the coverage remains applicable on a legal liability basis, but what the direct excess insurance does is this: coverage applies without regard to the legal liability of the insured for loss to a customer's auto on an excess basis over any other collectible insurance. As an example, if the customer's car had suffered damage through no fault of the insured, and the customer's own auto policy then paid for the damage with the customer paying his deductible, the garagekeepers direct excess coverage would apply, and the insured could pay the customer the deductible.

But in this instance, you say that the insured is liable for the damage. This means that the insured's garagekeepers coverage will pay for the fire damage (if he has the proper cause of loss coverage) based on the liability of the insured, and the direct excess option is not going to affect this payment. Both the amount of damage done to the customer's auto and the deductible paid by the customer will be paid by the garagekeepers coverage since that is the sum for which the insured is liable.

Garagekeepers Coverage—Repossessed Vehicle

Our insured is an auto repair facility that performed work on an auto and then released the car to the owner upon presentation of a check for full payment of services rendered, but the check bounced. Our insured then legally repossessed the car. The owner subsequently paid all damages and then sued the insured alleging theft, collision-type damages and loss of use of the car.

The insurer is denying defense and coverage for this lawsuit based on the allegation of theft and its interpretation that the vehicle was not left in the insured's care, as required for garagekeepers coverage to apply. It is my contention that this was a legal repossession and so the allegation of theft is baseless. Regarding the phrase "left in the insured's care," my contention is that since legal tender was not offered initially, at the point in time when the insured lawfully repossessed the vehicle, it became "left in the insured's care" until proper legal tender could be made.

Would the garagekeepers coverage apply in this situation?

Texas Subscriber

We agree with you about the theft allegation. There is an exclusion due to theft under the garagekeepers coverage, but since the insured legally repossessed the car, the insurer can not reasonably call this incident a theft. But, that is really a legal question and we cannot answer legal questions. You may want to consult with an attorney who is familiar with the laws in your area.

The question of coverage under the terms of the garagekeepers insurance depends on the meaning of the phrase "left in the insured's care", and whether there is a covered cause of loss in this event.

The insurer makes a good case for the car not being left in the insured's care since there was no hint on the part of the owner voluntarily leaving the car with the insured. Usually, when you leave something in another's care, you do so voluntarily. On the other hand, the garagekeepers form does not define "left in the insured's care." The dictionary defines "leave" as "to cause or allow to be or remain in a specified condition" and "to permit to be or remain subject to another's action or control."

The insured can certainly make the case that, due to the bounced check, the owner, in effect, caused or permitted the car to be subject to the insured's action or control. The insured repaired the car and had a right to be paid for the service; that was agreed to by both the insured and the owner. By not paying the bill, the owner reneged on the agreement, leaving the insured with the right to repossess the car, to make it subject to his control until the bill was paid. The insured legally repossessed the car according to what you say, so the state obviously recognizes his right to subject the car to his control.

The bottom line is that there may be enough ambiguity over the meaning of the phrase "left in the insured's care" to, at the very least, require the insurer to defend the insured in this lawsuit. And, if the lawsuit determines that the insured legally must pay for the loss to the car while the car was left in his care, there is no exclusion under garagekeepers coverage that would prevent such payment by the insurer. And, of course, for garagekeepers coverage, "loss" does include loss of use.

As to a covered cause of loss, the insured has to have chosen comprehensive coverage, which applies to any cause of loss except collision. Comprehensive coverage would include the type of loss claimed in this incident.

Golf Cart Considered a Covered Auto?

We have a client insured under a garage policy and this includes the physical damage coverage for loss to covered autos. During a recent storm, the insured's parking lot was flooded and his golf cart was damaged by the rising water. The definition of auto includes a land motor vehicle. Would the garage policy pay for the damage to the golf cart?

Hawaii Subscriber

According to the definition of auto on the garage form, a golf cart would be included in this category; it is a land motor vehicle. As long as the insured has chosen the applicable covered auto designation symbol for the physical damage coverage and applicable cause of loss (comprehensive coverage or specified causes of loss coverage), the coverage is there for this claim. There are no exclusions or conditions on the garage form that would prevent the coverage.

Hired Auto Physical Damage Coverage Question

Can you explain hired auto coverage under the garage policy? How is hired auto physical damage covered under the garage form? And, is the garage form primary coverage for the hired car?

Alabama Subscriber

Symbol 28, hired autos only, is used to provide coverage for those autos that the named insured leases, hires, rents or borrows. This does not include any auto that the named insured leases, hires, rents, or borrows from an employee, a partner, or a member of a limited liability company.

For hired auto physical damage coverage, any auto that the named insured lease, hires, rents, or borrows is deemed to be a covered auto that the named insured owns. This means that the physical damage coverage is primary coverage should any damage occur to such an auto. Of course, even though the physical damage coverage is primary, if there is any other coverage form that applies on the same primary basis, the payment for the damage is paid on a pro-rate basis.

Note that liability coverage for a hired auto is still on an excess basis over any other collectible insurance since the auto is not owned by the named insured.

Medical Payments Available for Injuries Due to Nonowned Trailer?

Our insured is an auto dealership. He was using a dealership owned vehicle to haul a nonowned trailer with a float on it in a local parade. The insured driver strayed from the parade route and struck an overhead tree limb, resulting in the passengers being thrown overboard from the float.

The question is whether or not the auto medical payments coverage applies. The garage policy has symbol 22, owned autos only, for its description of covered autos. Symbol 22 is used for the liability coverage, but the med pay endorsement indicates that coverage in this type of occurrence is for "covered autos", without further defining what that term means. We are confused. My inclination is to provide coverage for the medical payments since the vehicle is a covered auto for liability purposes, but I am not sure since the med pay endorsement does not clarify what is meant by a covered auto. What is your opinion?

Ohio Subscriber

We agree with your opinion about the med pay coverage. The nonowned trailer was a covered auto since symbol 22 designates as a covered auto owned autos and trailers not owned by the named insured while attached to owned power units. This designation does say that the coverage for nonowned trailers is for liability coverage, but it does not say "for liability coverage only". A case can be made that nonowned trailers are considered covered autos, and that is the important point. As such, the trailer in this case, as a covered auto, is included in the scope of med pay coverage.

Besides, based on your description of this accident, it appears that a liability claim could be made by those who were injured. Med pay is not based on liability, of course, but one of the purposes of med pay is to pay reasonable expenses upfront in order to possibly prevent a liability claim from developing at some later date. So, if the insurer in this case agrees to pay medical payments claims and there is no valid exclusion on your policy to prevent the payments, it makes sense to proceed.

Permissive Driver Dispute under Garage Policy

Our insured is a car dealer. He allowed his son to use a covered auto even though the son was a driver excluded by name under the terms of the garage policy. The son then allowed a third party to drive the car and he caused an accident in which a fatality occurred.

We are wondering if the driver, who got permission to drive the car from an excluded driver, is considered an insured for purposes of defense and liability coverage. Some in our office say yes and others disagree. What is your opinion?

California Subscriber

The thing to know in this instance is whether the third party knew if he was allowed to drive the car or not. The who is an insured clause on the garage form states that anyone using a covered car with the permission of the named insured is considered an insured. If the third party thought it was permissible to use the vehicle because he thought the son had permission to use the car and the son passed the permission on to him, then the third party would be considered a permissible driver and an insured for coverage purposes. Unless the third party knew without any doubt that there was no way he was allowed to use the car—for example, if the dealer insured told him or told the son in the presence of the third party that no one else was allowed to drive the car, or if the third party knew the son was not allowed to drive the car but was doing so anyway—then there has to be a presumption that the third party reasonably thought he could use the car just because the one driving it said he could do so.

The fact that the insurer had excluded the son from being an insured under the garage policy does not alter the point that the third party may have had reasonable justification for thinking he had authentic permission to drive the car.

Physical Damage Deductible
— Commercial Auto Policy

One of the auto dealers I represent carries specified perils coverage for auto physical damage on garage coverage form CA 00 05 03 06. He sustained a loss under this coverage section, and I want to be sure that the deductible is applied properly. In reading the form, I believe that a deductible applies only to losses when caused by theft, mischief, or vandalism. However, this just doesn't seem right. How should the deductible be applied?

Louisiana Subscriber

Section IV, physical damage coverage, on form CA 00 05 states that the comprehensive or specified causes of loss coverage deductible applies only to loss caused by theft or mischief or vandalism or all perils. This is obviously confusing language since it lumps comprehensive coverage with the specified causes of loss coverage. What you need to do is read the clarifying information found in the garage declarations, CA DS 09 03 06.

In item two of the declarations (the schedule of coverages and covered autos), under the physical damage specified causes of loss coverage clause, it states that the deductible is applied to each covered auto for loss caused by mischief or vandalism. Then, it refers the insured to item seven of the declarations for dealers autos. Item seven declares that for comprehensive or specified causes of loss, the deductible is applied for each covered auto for loss caused by theft or mischief or vandalism subject to a maximum deductible for all such loss in any one event. Or, item seven goes on, the deductible applies for all perils subject to a maximum deductible for all such loss in any one event.

What this means is that the insurer is allowing the insured to choose not only which type cause of loss will apply (comprehensive or specified causes of loss), but also whether the deductible will apply only to loss caused by theft, mischief, or vandalism, or whether the deductible will apply to loss caused by all perils, which would include theft, mischief, and vandalism as well as any other cause of loss (except collision). Your insured may have chosen his physical damage deductible to apply only to theft, mischief, or vandalism. Check the garage declarations to be sure.

Physical Damage Loss Raises Coverage Question

We provided a garage coverage form to an auto dealer, with a policy term of May 1, 2004 to May 1, 2005. The auto dealer switched his insurance coverage to another carrier as of the May 1, 2005 date. The dealer then discovered the theft of an inventory vehicle on June 3, 2005 and the police were notified. The last date that the insured can physically place the vehicle on the lot is March 2, 2005. We do not believe that there is any evidence that the vehicle was stolen during the policy period of our policy. If a claim is made against our policy, would this loss be compensable?

New York Subscriber

The garage policy does not address the issue of coverage when physical damages losses occur as it does with the liability coverage part of the policy. Liability coverage applies if the injury or damage occurs during the policy period, but the physical damage insuring agreement simply talks about paying for a loss. However, it is reasonable to believe that a loss to a covered auto would have to occur within the policy period for coverage to exist.

In what may be a guideline for you to follow in this instance, the prevailing rule (majority rule) is that property damage occurs at the time the damage is discovered or when it manifests itself. Since physical damage is, in reality, damage to the property of the insured, it makes sense to apply the prevailing rule and say that, in this case, the damage to or loss of the insured's property occurred when it was discovered—June 3, 2005. That would put the loss outside your policy period.

Besides, the insured has to prove he has suffered a covered loss before the insurer is required to pay for such loss. Unless the insured can prove he lost the car during your policy period, the claim should be handled by the carrier that succeeded you on this coverage.

Products of Named Insured Covered by Garage Policy?

Our insured is a garage business and sells items such as tires, batteries, and other automobile-related things. If the insured sells a product to a customer and the product subsequently causes injuries or damages, will the garage policy apply to a claim against the insured? We know there is a defective products exclusion on the garage policy and we are wondering about its extent.

Kansas Subscriber

There is a defective products exclusion on the garage policy, but that applies only to property damage to any of the named insured's products if caused by a defect existing in the product at the time it was transferred to another. In other words, this exclusion applies only to damage to the product of the insured. If the product causes damage to another person's property or causes injury to someone, the resulting claim is not affected by the products exclusion. As an example, if the insured sells a defective tire to a customer and later there is a blowout and the customer's car is damaged in a resulting collision, the products exclusion on the garage policy eliminates coverage for the defective tire, but does not affect the liability coverage for the damaged auto.

For your information, there is an endorsement that gives the insured coverage for his defective products if such a coverage is desired. CA 25 01 12 93, broad form products coverage, changes the liability coverage of the insured under the garage policy by eliminating the defective products exclusion. However, there is a limitation to the coverage offered by this endorsement. Subject to the each accident limit of insurance, the coverage provided by CA 25 01 only applies to that amount of property damage to the named insured's products that exceeds $250 for any one accident. The insured has, in effect, a $250 deductible for this coverage, but the endorsement does offer some coverage to the insured for damage to his products.

Theft of Personal Property Covered by GKLL?

Our garage coverage form provides coverage for the theft of personal property of customers from autos in the care of the insured; this is included under the terms of the garagekeepers (GKLL) section of the policy. "Customers' personal property" is defined simply as personal property of the customer left in the car of the customer, except specified certain items.

The claim revolves around an employee of a business who left his personal auto at our insured's service shop for some repair work. The personal vehicle contained several thousand dollars worth of parts that were owned by the customer's employer. The parts were stolen and a claim made against our insured. So, can the employer's items be deemed to be the customer's personal property?

West Virginia Subscriber

The way your policy defines customer's personal property, that is, personal property left in the customer's car, is a very broad definition; it does not limit the personal property to that of the customer only. The property in this instance was personal property (albeit business personal property) and it was left in the customer's car, so unless there was some limitation that would limit the coverage in some way (for example, the list of specified items), or some exclusion that might be applicable, coverage for the parts is there.

Now, you should check to see how the coverage insuring agreement is worded. For example, the standard GKLL coverage is based on the legally liability of the insured. The insured has to be legally liable for the loss to the customer's auto or its equipment before coverage kicks in. And, there is an exclusion of coverage for theft by the named insured or his employees. So, check the policy you have and see if the insuring agreement has been met and see if there are any exclusions that might apply to this claim.

Faulty Work Exclusion under Garage Policy

Our insured, an auto repair shop, has an ISO garage coverage form CA 00 05 03 06. Recently a customer's car windows were damaged when an overspray of paint got on the windows of their vehicle. In attempting to remove the paint, the windows were scratched.

The company has denied the claim, citing exclusion 13, "This insurance does not apply to...'property damage' to 'work you performed' if the 'property damage' results from any part of the work itself or from the parts, materials or equipment used in connection with the work." Is this correct?

North Carolina Subscriber

The insurer may say that the faulty work exclusion applies but we don't agree with that approach. That exclusion (as well as the care, custody, or control exclusion, which might be applied by the insurer) is for the liability coverage section of the garage policy. What has to be examined with respect to this claim is the garagekeepers coverage in the garage policy. This is so because the damage occurred while the property was left in the insured's care for servicing.

The garagekeepers coverage is for the sums that the insured legally must pay as damages for loss to a customer's auto left in the care of the insured and due to a covered cause of loss. So, coverage depends on what type of cause of loss the insured purchased. For example, if the insured purchased just collision coverage or specified causes of loss coverage, this type of claim is not covered. Paint overspray and scratching windows are losses that are covered under the comprehensive cause of loss. If the insured has that type of coverage, this claim is covered.

There is a faulty work exclusion under the garagekeepers coverage section of the garage policy, but that applies to completed operations faulty work. For example, if the insured did the spray paint job and then after it was finished, the paint chipped or looked splotchy, that would not be covered by the garagekeepers coverage. However in this case, the damage occurred while the insured was actually performing operations on the car and a claim for that type of that damage is not excluded.

Work You Performed Exclusion Prevents Garage Liability Coverage?

Our insured is involved in the work of adding truck bodies to chassis. Sometimes the body will be installed on a truck cab and chassis owned by a customer and at other times, the insured will acquire the cab and chassis and then do the installation on his own property.

Recently, the insured sold a truck and body to another party. For some reason, the cab and chassis were temporarily titled to the insured. The body failed and in turn, pulled the truck onto its side. The adjuster for the company has denied coverage for the claim citing the damage to your work exclusion. It is his position that the entire cab, chassis and body, was the work of the insured and the exclusion precludes any coverage for the property damage. Is this correct?

Pennsylvania Subscriber

If the insured had title to the cab and chassis when the accident occurred, this would be considered as the property of the insured. That means the garage liability policy (or any liability policy) will not provide coverage for damage to the property. Liability forms do not provide coverage for damage to the named insured's property.

As for the truck and body that were sold to a customer, they would be considered the product of the named insured based on the definition of "your product" which is: the goods or products the named insured makes or sells in a garage business. The garage policy excludes liability coverage for property damage to any of the named insured's products if the property damage is caused by a defect existing in the products at the time it was transferred to another. So, if the damage was caused by a defect in the body, such as the failure of the body noted by you, that damage is not covered due to the defective products exclusion.

The work you performed exclusion on the garage form applies if the property damage results from any part of the work itself, or from the parts, materials, or equipment used in connection with the work. This exclusion applies only to the work that the named insured did. If he only worked on the cab and chassis and his work caused damage to the cab and chassis, that damage is excluded. But, if his work caused damage to something else, something that the insured did not work on, then that damage is covered. So, in this case, unless the insured performed work on the body and truck, the exclusion used by the adjuster is not the correct one to prevent coverage for the claim.

COMMERCIAL PROPERTY

Surface Water and Mudflow Cause Builders Risk Loss

A torrential downpour washed out ground on a graded area at a construction site. As a result, the slope had to be re-excavated and re-prepared. Our insured had a builders risk policy that included coverage for site preparation if the re-excavation is necessary due to a covered cause of loss. Landslide is excluded on the form, but flood, including rapid runoff of surface water and mudslide/mudflow, are covered. Would this loss be covered?

Tennessee Subscriber

Mudslide is defined on the policy as "a river or flow of liquid mud caused by or resulting from...flooding." *Landslide* is not defined on the policy, so we must turn to a dictionary for its lay definition: "the unusually rapid downward movement of a mass of rock, earth, or artificial fill on a slope." (*Merriam-Webster Online*.)

From the description you presented, it appears that rapid accumulation and runoff of surface water—caused by the torrential downpour—and/or mudflow caused the damage. The dictionary definition of *landslide* does not include any mention of water or rainfall as related to it, as is the case in the situation you described.

Expense of Cleaning Undamaged Apartments Covered

I am a public adjuster working on several apartment claims in the New Orleans area as a result of Hurricane Katrina. The insured has policies similar to the ISO Building and Personal Property Coverage form, CP 00 10 04 02, with a Special Causes of Loss form, CP 10 30 04 02, as well as a Business Income (And Extra Expense) form, CP 00 30 04 02. The coverage is written blanket on the property that has approximately twenty buildings, all of which sustained significant exterior damage. The buildings contain about 380 individual apartments, and all but 150 sustained varying degrees of wind and water damage. The remaining 150 units have no detectable physical damage. As a result of the overall damage to the property, all 380 units had to be vacated.

In order to reoccupy the 150 undamaged units, the owner will have to completely repaint, clean the carpets, and generally clean the apartments,

just as they would do before renting to a new tenant. The cost would be about $2,500 per apartment. The adjuster said the cost would not be covered because there was no direct, physical damage to these units, as required by the policy. Given the extensive damage to every building, we think it is arguable that there is physical damage to each building, and these units should be addressed as property damage.

If it is not property damage, would the cost be considered extra expense under the business income coverage? It is clearly an additional expense caused by the storm that would have to be incurred before the units can be rented again.

Texas Subscriber

Based on your description of events, the costs to prepare the undamaged units for rental should be paid.

While the policy does specify that loss is payable for "direct physical loss or damage to Covered Property," the units in question have not sustained direct physical loss or damage, so this portion of the policy would not be triggered. However, the general conditions section of the policy does discuss consequential loss. This provision states that the insurance provided will apply to covered loss or damage that emanates from the initial covered cause of loss. The buildings in which these undamaged units are situated were damaged, necessitating that all units be evacuated. An argument might be made that the refurbishing of undamaged units emanated from the initial damage. This is the most difficult argument to make, but, since the buildings were actually damaged directly, coverage for the consequential loss of refurbishing the undamaged units could be made.

The rental value provision states that the company will give "due consideration to the continuation of normal charges and expenses" to the extent that they are necessary to resume business operations. If the apartments were not made ready, they would not be able to be rented and business income would be affected. This type of work should be considered a normal and necessary continuing expense.

The final and most convincing reason for payment lies in the extra expense provision. The insuring agreement states that the carrier will pay for "actual and necessary Extra Expense that you sustain due to direct physical loss of or damage to property at premises…for which Extra Expense Limits of Insurance are stated in the Declarations." The coverage requires only to damage to property at premises. This condition is clearly met by virtue of the damage to the buildings, which are located at the same premises as the individual units. The insured must spruce up the units before renting them again, which is a necessary extra expense. Either this provision or the rental value may apply—but not both, since an expense cannot be both normal and extra.

ISO Businessowners Policy Does Not Require Insured to Own Building

I am having an argument with an underwriter on a specialty program for a deli-style sandwich shop in regards to "covered property" definitions. My client is a tenant in three locations. The client is insured on a split basis for buildings and business personal property. The company's businessowners form, under covered property—buildings, includes "permanently installed fixtures, machinery and equipment, outdoor fixtures, personal property owned and used to maintain/service the building, including floor coverings and appliances used for refrigerating, ventilating, cooking, dishwashing...." The insured has all of these items. We have been splitting these out from the business personal property and insuring for a different amount under building coverage.

The underwriter says we cannot do this because the insured "does not own the building." I have read the policy, and it does not say the insured has to own the building for this coverage.

North Carolina Subscriber

The ISO businessowners policy does not include any wording specifying that the named insured must own the building in order to insure property under the building section. The tenant must have an insurable interest in all the property he insures and that would include these types of permanent fixtures. While the provision for "personal property used to service the building" is typically thought to apply to equipment (such as lawn mowers and washing machines) that are moveable yet owned by the landlord (building owner) and used to service the building, the policy does not limit that coverage to the building owner. Likewise, building coverage for fixtures and permanently installed machinery and equipment are not limited to the building owner.

Having said that, the carrier is free to adopt its own underwriting rules. The carrier may have chosen not to offer such coverage under the building provision, and it has every right to do so. But, the actual policy (unless it differs from the ISO form) does not require that building coverage be written only for building owners.

Does Retooling Locks Qualify as an Extra Expense?

Our insured is a vending company with an Extra Expense Coverage form, CP 00 50 04 02. The keys to all vending machines at all locations were stolen, and all the locks on the machines had to be retooled or changed. We do not insure the machines or stock in them, just the premises. The insurer says there is no physical damage to property, so there is no coverage. What are your thoughts?

Ohio Subscriber

Because the vending machine locations are not considered insured premises, the CP 00 50 04 02 would not respond to this loss. The form promises to insure "damage to property at premises which are described in the Declarations." The loss also would not be triggered for the CP 00 10 04 02's (Building and Personal Property Coverage form) requirement to prevent further loss. So, the retooling would not be a covered loss.

Failure of Grease Trap Not Covered

My client has a one-year-old grease trap, two holding tanks, and a large leech field. It appears that the grease trap failed and caused the entire system to fail. Would this loss be covered on the CP 00 10 04 02, Building and Personal Property Coverage form or the equipment breakdown endorsement?

Massachusetts Subscriber

There are several areas that may preclude coverage for this loss:

1. The commercial property form includes, under property not covered, "Underground pipes, flues, or drains." Due to this limitation, the underground pipes/drains included within the septic system would not be insured.

2. The exclusion of underground piping would not necessarily preclude coverage for the leech field, although underground pipes that are a part of it would not be covered. Your description of the loss does not provide sufficient information about what caused the grease trap to fail. For example, if it was just too small to handle the amount of grease, there would be no coverage because there would be no occurrence or accident. If it simply did not work because of faulty design, also excluded. However, if it were mechanical and broke down—ruptured, burst, broke apart—the occurrence would meet the definition of "accident" on the equipment breakdown endorsement. However, the endorsement states that sewer piping and underground vessels or

piping are not "covered equipment," so that would preclude coverage under the endorsement.

3. A plugged up leech field does not necessarily equate to a damaged leech field. If the problem can be resolved by cleaning out the grease trap, that would fall within the area of maintenance.

4. If there are no pipes in the leech field, and it simply is a series of various sizes of gravel and filtering earth, then it would be land, which is also excluded from property coverage.

Based on the information you provided, this loss would not be covered.

How Should Parking Lot Be Covered under AAIS Businessowners Form?

We have an insured who is asking that we provide a $300,000 property limit for a newly acquired parking lot (not a parking garage) adjacent to the insured's building. The insured is also asking that we name the bank as a mortgagee in relation to this limit, as mandated by the bank. It is not clear to me if this is building coverage, fixtures coverage within the definition of building, building personal property in the open, or simply land. Land is excluded from the AAIS Businessowners form, BP-200 Ed. 1, for property coverage.

I suspect that much of the $300,000 is for the land itself and not for the asphalt or concrete car stops atop the asphalt, and therefore not covered. Can you provide guidance on how we should view the parking lot itself and related car stops?

Wisconsin Subscriber

You present a very interesting question, the resolution of which may entail some conversation on your part with the underwriters and/or the bank.

You are correct that the AAIS BP-200 Ed. 1 does not cover land. However, unlike the ISO building and personal property coverage form, paved surfaces are not excluded. Therefore, the businessowners form should apply to them.

The paved parking lot would be an outdoor fixture, which is considered under the building category on the form.

Despite the fact that paved surfaces are not excluded, it may be prudent to notify the underwriter that a parking lot is being insured and ask that it be listed for coverage. In that way, there would be no question as to its being insured should a loss occur.

The difficult items that must be considered are the value of the parking lot and the causes of loss that would typically damage it.

The insured wants to cover the parking lot for $300,000. The businessowners form is written on a replacement cost basis, so it may be prudent for the insured to obtain an estimate from a paving contractor as to what the cost to replace the lot would be—with the same type and quality of materials but excluding land value. If this amount differs greatly from the $300,000, the insured may want to negotiate the amount of insurance the bank requires. The bank needs to understand that the land cannot be insured and should not be included in the value.

It's interesting to consider what causes of loss most typically would affect a parking lot. Limitations or exclusions on the businessowners form include the fact that collapse of paved surfaces must result from a specified peril as defined on the form. In addition, covered collapse losses to paved surfaces must result directly from collapse of a building or structure. Mere caving in of a parking lot separate from a building collapse would not fall within this narrow description of collapse.

Sinkhole collapse must be caused by the action of water on limestone or similar material, so a sinkhole in the lot might or might not be covered. The cost of filling sinkholes is excluded.

Earth movement is excluded on the form, as are surface water pressing against paved surfaces and settling, cracking, shrinking, or expansion of pavements.

The bottom line is that many of the causes of loss that we typically think of as damaging a paved parking lot are excluded from coverage. Although the same exclusions exist for other types of property, they are particularly onerous for a parking lot. Therefore, it may be prudent for the insured and the bank to consider such issues before requiring/purchasing $300,000 of insurance.

One Deductible Applies to One Occurrence

Under an ISO Building and Personal Property Coverage form, CP 00 10 04 02, with a Special Causes of Loss form, CP 10 30 04 02, we have several school buildings insured at different locations within the county. A lightning storm damaged several schools. The insured is requesting one deductible since damage was rendered by one storm. The carrier, though, is applying separate deductibles to each location damaged since they are miles apart. Is the carrier applying the deductibles correctly?

Delaware Subscriber

The CP 00 10 specifically states that the deductible is applied only once per occurrence, regardless of how many subjects of insurance are damaged. So, the question goes to the meaning of occurrence. One storm that damaged multiple buildings, even at different locations, is one occurrence, and therefore only one deductible should apply.

ISO does permit the use of per location deductibles, so if a policy featured such deductibles, multiple deductibles would be allowed.

Dispersal of Toxins Pollution or Explosion Loss?

Under an ISO Building and Personal Property Coverage form, CP 00 10 04 02, with a Special Causes of Loss form, CP 10 30 04 02, a loss occurred when a chemical reaction caused an uncontrolled release of a highly toxic compound. The insured's fume hood had to be replaced due to the toxins that gathered on the hood. The insured is requesting coverage under the explosion peril. The insurer believes this is a pollution loss. Who is correct?

Delaware Subscriber

The pollution exclusion of CP 00 10 excludes pollution as follows:

Discharge, dispersal, seepage, migration, release or escape of "pollutants" unless the discharge, dispersal, seepage, migration, release or escape is itself caused by any of the "specified causes of loss." But if discharge, dispersal, seepage, migration, release or escape of "pollutants" results in a "specified causes of loss," we will pay for the loss or damage caused by that "specified causes of loss."

Your description of the loss states that toxins "gathered on the hood" from the release of toxins caused by a chemical reaction. Explosion is a specified cause of loss. So, if the pollutant dispersal was caused by an explosion, coverage would be triggered despite the fact that the pollutants are involved. The question is, does a chemical reaction causing an "uncontrolled release" of a compound qualify as an explosion?

"Explosion" is not defined on the policy, and courts in various jurisdictions have interpreted it differently. However, a common theme runs through many of the cases: explosion is described as a sudden and violent release or an active force that suddenly and violently exerts itself. Your description does not provide enough information to determine whether the mixture of chemicals was explosive in nature or just caused fumes, which carried the pollutants to the hood. If the reaction were explosive in nature, the claim would be covered. If not, it would not qualify as an explosion, so coverage would not be triggered.

Motor Scooters and Motorcycles Held for Sale Covered under Commercial Property Form

We contend that motor scooters, motorcycles, and similar vehicles were never intended to be insured under a building and personal property coverage form and that they should be covered under a dealers policy—as if they were automobiles—since they are licensed for road use.

Since there is a boom in dealers selling these vehicles, we want to be certain of our position on the matter.

Puerto Rico Subscriber

The CP 00 10 10 90, under property not covered, states that vehicles or self-propelled machines that are licensed for use on public roadways are not covered unless they are not autos and are being held for sale or warehoused. Based on this, motor scooters and motorcycles are covered under the form while they are held for sale. Once sold, coverage ceases.

Bowling Pins and Pin-Setting Machines Real or Business Personal Property?

Our insured is a bowling alley, and we would like to know if the lanes and modular pin-setting apparatus should be considered real or business personal property under the CP 00 10 04 02.

Kentucky Subscriber

The lane and pin-setting system, which you described as modular, may be considered a fixture or machinery and equipment. A fixture may be covered as either building or business personal property on the CP 00 10 04 02. Since fixtures fall under both categories, either may be selected pending circumstances of the specific situation.

One court has ruled that pin-setting machines were business personal property in *Rothermich v. Union Planters National Bank*. A major line of reasoning in the case was intent, in that the lease agreement for the property classified the pin-setting equipment as personal property. However, absent such intentional classification in a legal document, the equipment you described could be covered as either building or business personal property.

Extended Period of Indemnity under a Builders Risk Policy

How does the business income extended period of indemnity work with a builders risk policy?

Colorado Subscriber

Time element insurance may be written with on a building under construction. According to the ISO manual rules, the declarations must state that the risk is under construction and must indicate the contemplated date of occupancy. The carrier must be notified and the rate adjusted when the construction is completed.

Business income insurance is written by attaching CP 00 30, Business Income (And Extra Expense), or CP 00 32, Business Income (Without Extra Expense) to the builders risk coverage form.

The ISO business income forms include a provision for a thirty-day extended period of indemnity. This time period may be extended by activating the optional coverage on the business income declarations and paying the applicable additional premium.

Decrease in Sale Price Not Covered by Business Income Policy

We have a commercial insured who is going through a large fire claim, including a business income loss. To complicate matters, the building that burned was in the process of being sold. The insured asked that if he suffers a loss in the sale of the building as a result of the fire, would he have coverage under his Business Income form, CP 00 30 04 02, in the event the final purchase price is less than prior to the claim?

Michigan Subscriber

Business income coverage responds to the loss of business income that an insured incurs due to a suspension of operations that is caused when property at the premises is damaged by a covered cause of loss. It is unlikely that business income insurance would respond to merely a decrease in the sale price of a building that was damaged by a covered cause of loss.

The sale of a building would not typically be part of the company's normal operations or a part of the stream of business income. Even though income from the sale of a building would bring revenue to the insured company, it is difficult to see where a decrease in the building's sale price, due to covered damage,

would cause a suspension of operations. After all, the building was to be sold even before it was damaged so probably was not integral to operations.

In addition, the Special Causes of Loss form, CP 10 30 04 02, excludes coverage for any increase of loss caused by or resulting from "suspension, lapse or cancellation of any license, lease or contract" unless the suspension, lapse or cancellation is directly caused by the suspension of operations. Again, since the building was already in the process of being sold, it is difficult to see where its damage could suspend operations.

If the building were tenant-occupied, and if the tenancy rate plummeted because of the property damage, and the lack of tenancy caused the sale price to drop, the insured business could be entitled to recover the loss of rental income from the time of damage until the new sale price is finalized. The recovery would be limited by the period of restoration, as defined in the policy.

Also, if the insured were in the business of managing and selling properties, and if the damage to one of its buildings resulted in a loss of income, coverage might be negotiated.

In general, however, the property policy insuring the building should indemnify the insured for damage to the building, not the business income coverage form.

Underwriter Does Not Have Obligation to Ask about Noncovered Building Contents

Our insured added a garage to her commercial property policy, but for building coverage only. Some contents were stolen from the garage, and the carrier is denying coverage for the contents because contents is not listed on the policy. Does the underwriter have an obligation to ask about contents? Is there any way to find coverage?

Ohio Subscriber

An underwriter does not have an obligation to ask about contents. If the carrier did an inspection, there may be room for an argument, but otherwise, there is no legal obligation for underwriter to question contents needs.

Since the commercial property declarations page requires contents to be listed, there would be no coverage for the garage contents.

Pumpkins Excluded by Crop Exclusion

We have an insured who had a large number of pumpkins that they bought from farmers to sell during a fall festival. The pumpkins were stored outside. A large unexpected snow storm in October ruined the pumpkins. The insurer is denying coverage for damage to the pumpkins based on this exclusion in their property form:

The following property while outside of buildings:

(1)   Grain, hay, straw or other crops;

(2) Trees, shrubs or plants (other than "stock" of trees, shrubs or plants), except as provided in the Coverage Extensions

We believe that this exclusion does not fit our insured's situation. The pumpkins are personal property being held for sale by a retail store that are no different than bicycles or other products being stored outside while being held for sale.

What is your opinion?

Kentucky Subscriber

With a strict reading of the policy, the pumpkins are included in this exclusion. Notice that trees, shrubs, and plants in (2) are followed by the qualifier "other than 'stock,'" while grain, hay, straw, and other crops are not. Pumpkins fit the dictionary definition of crop: "a plant or animal or plant or animal product that can be grown and harvested extensively for profit or subsistence." (Merriam-Webster Online). Thus, while pumpkins could be considered personal property being held for sale, they are also crops and subject to this exclusion.

Insurer Responsible for Fines and Other Costs due to Delay in Repair

Our insured owns an older, ten story building in a downtown metropolitan area. Several of the floors are rented to a single major client. They had a water loss damaging several floors, with damages in excess of $140,000. Additionally, one smoke detector was shorted out on a lower floor, making part of the fire panel inoperable. The fire panel has been red-tagged ever since. As the fire panel is an older model, and I believe only produced for one year, replacement parts are not available for this unit. Both the insured's contractor and an engineering firm hired by the insurance carrier have attempted to locate a used part to repair the fire system. The red tag puts the building in code violation. To date repairs have not been

authorized by the carrier. Should the Fire Marshall choose, the building could be shut down; the owners could be fined or possibly be placed on a twenty-four hour fire watch until the time the panel repairs have been made.

Who would be responsible for this cost?

As replacement parts could not be found to bring the building to code, the insured's contractor estimated repair/replacement cost at $950,000. The carrier's engineer stated that he had located a part that would work with the fire panel that costs $35. Using the part with the insured's current fire panel has not been UL approved, and the manufacturer could not recommend or approve its use with the panel. The contractor said that if this method was used, they would still have to place a "yellow tag" on the building. The carrier said that if the part works, they have fulfilled their responsibility of making the insured whole, even with the yellow tag. The carrier did not believe they would have any legal responsibility using a non-UL or manufacturer approved method of repairing. The contractor presented a proposal to the insured offering to make the repairs, leaving the panel with a yellow tag and demanding an indemnification agreement that they were not responsible for any future damages or liability. The insured agreed to their demand and signed the agreement. The contractor has become leery of doing the work and has not scheduled the work. The insured has contacted other fire system contractors, and they say they would also yellow tag the fire panel. Would such repairs make the insured whole? Is the carrier responsible for bringing the building up to code since the current system (new or used) is not available? Wouldn't the insurance carrier be responsible for repairs to remove the red or yellow tag and bring it back to a green tag?

Ohio Subscriber

Based on the situation you describe, the insured is not made whole if the fire panel does not function as it did prior to the loss. Since the panel was not red or yellow tagged prior to the loss, the insured would not be made whole by the repairs suggested. The insurer would be responsible for fines or other costs due to the delay in repairing the panel, but it would probably be difficult to enforce their payment.

Loss of Use of Football Helmets Excluded

Insured is school district with commercial property form providing coverage for "direct physical loss." Football helmets were stored in a building that sustained fire loss. Helmets were cleaned to assure no smoke odor. Inspection of helmet reveals no sign of physical damage and expert opines heat not intense in area of helmet storage to cause physical damage. The manufacturer refuses to certify helmets due to exposure to fire loss and potential damage. School is without use of helmets without required certification. Insurer claims loss of use of property absent direct physical loss is not a covered loss. Do you agree?

Texas Subscriber

Yes, we do agree with the insurer. Since there is no physical loss to the helmets, the only loss is their use. The ISO Building and Personal Property form, CP 10 30 04 02, states, "We will not pay for loss or damage caused by or resulting from...loss of use."

Does Proximate Cause Doctrine Apply When Three Covered Losses Act Together?

I have researched proximate cause and efficient proximate cause issues and still have not found anything directly relating to my question. Usually these subjects deal with covered and noncovered causes of loss acting together. My situation involves three covered causes of loss acting together.

My insured's business is located in Florida. During a windstorm the wind blew a tree onto a powerline. The powerline arced and caused a power surge, which damaged insured electrical equipment. There is no boiler and machinery coverage. The policy is an ISO Building and Personal Property Coverage form, CP 00 10 04 02.

The carrier finds that the proximate cause of loss is wind and is applying the 5 percent wind deductible, which absorbs the entire loss and results in no payment. Since both "falling objects" and "damage caused by artificially generated electric current" (the most dominant, direct cause of the loss) are covered causes of loss (though not "named perils") wouldn't the electrical surge be the efficient proximate cause of loss and therefore subject the loss to the "other perils" deductible?

What would be a good example of dependent causes of loss versus independent causes of loss?

Florida Subscriber

You pose an interesting question because, as you state, most of the materials on proximate cause do address scenarios involving both covered and noncovered causes of loss and not those where all causes of loss are covered. However, it is our opinion that the proximate cause doctrine would still apply. The wind knocking the tree over set the whole chain of events in motion. Without that action, there would have been no electrical arcing or power surge. And, that is an example of dependent causes of loss. Without the first action, the other actions would not have happened. Independent causes of loss are those usually addressed by the concurrent causation doctrine. They occur at the same time, but may have nothing to do with each other. For instance, a car may crash into a burning building. Both the car and the fire cause damage to the building, but one cause of loss is not dependent on the other. The car crash could still occur and cause damage even if there was no fire, and vice versa.

Inclusion of Contents Coverage Not a Factor in Loss

Our client owns a convenience store and leases it out to a tenant but retains the rights to gas sale and profits. We insure the owner under a businessowners policy as a lessors risk for the real estate and the tenant under a separate businessowners for the operations. There was a fire, allegedly started by the tenant, which is under investigation. The owner is requesting loss of income, and the company says sure, only for the loss of rents. Obviously the owner says no because loss of income from the gas sale should also be included. The company says no, because contents coverage was not included on his businessowners policy. Who is right?

Ohio Subscriber

Whether the insured has contents insurance does not come into play. In order to recover business income for the loss, the insured would need to prove that the loss meets the requirements under the business income section of the businessowners form (e.g., operations were suspended due to a covered cause of loss). If the requirements are met, the gas sales should not be excluded.

Curbing around Sign Is Property Not Covered

Our insured had a decorative concrete curb around the sign at the front of their building. An unknown vehicle ran off the road and destroyed the curbing. The insurance adjuster denied the claim based on this provision from the Building and Personal Property Coverage form, CP 00 10 04 02:

2.   *Property not covered.*

d.   *Bridges, roadways, walks, patios or other paved surface.*

My feeling is that is should be considered an outdoor fixture. I feel that d. contemplates either vehicle traffic or pedestrian traffic, whereas the decorative curbing was intended to protect the sign it encircled.

Delaware Subscriber

The adjuster is correct, and the curbing is property not covered. It sounds as if it is similar to curbing on a road or driveway and intended to protect the sign from vehicles. It would be considered part of the roadway or another paved surface.

Decorative Fish Not Covered under Commercial Property Policy

Our insured is a restaurant that has a tropical fish tank along with tropical fish. The Insured suffered a power surge due to a lightning strike, which in turn caused the tank to shut down and the fish to die .The insurance carrier is not paying for the fish as "animals" are excluded. However, our argument is that the fish are actually decorative so therefore they should be covered. Furthermore, "animal" is not clearly defined in the policy.

Are you of the opinion, as we are, that tropical fish in this case are intended to be purely decorative? Is there an insurance definition of "animal" or "animals"?

Washington Subscriber

While there is not a specific insurance definition of "animal," of which we are aware, looking at the dictionary definition, a fish is an animal. *Merriam-Webster's* defines "fish" as "an aquatic animal."

The ISO CP 00 10 04 02 lists animals as property not covered, unless they are stock inside buildings. Since the fish are for decorative purposes only, they would not fit into the definition of "stock." The fish would not be covered.

Miscellaneous

CRIME

Theft of Clothing Covered as Employee Dishonesty?

Our insured has coverage under a CP 00 10 building and personal property form with covered causes of loss under CP 10 30, Special Form.

The policy also carries the CR 00 01 (10/90) employee dishonesty form. This is a retail clothing store. The store manager had been stealing items and reporting them in the computer system as "removed from inventory," which is a code reserved for damaged or liquidated inventory. This went on for two years before the insured caught on.

I know there is an exclusion under the CR 00 01 for Inventory Shortages, and I believe this loss is excluded. However, I would like another opinion before I make a final coverage decision.

Connecticut subscriber

Inventory shortages are excluded when the proof of the shortage is dependent on an inventory computation or profit and loss computation, neither of which is defined in the policy. Therefore, we go to the dictionary. Computation is defined as the act of computing, which is to determine by mathematical means. If your insured discovered the loss by way of such calculations, then indeed the loss is excluded.

But if the insured discovered and substantiated the loss some other way, a review of surveillance tapes or some such, then there would be coverage.

Changed Check Coding Results in Coverage Denial

Our insured has commercial crime coverage under form CR 00 21 07 02. An employee stole money by fraudulently issuing and cashing company checks from the insured company's pension plan.

The insurer has hired a forensic accountant to review the insured's books. Based on the forensic accountant's review, the insurer is declining to pay $7,719.49 of the loss. The reason given is that the original coding of the checks by the employee has been changed from the original code to an "employee theft code." This was done at the direction of the insured's accountant. The insured does not have a backup of its bookkeeping computer files with the original coding. The insurer said it will not pay without this original coding information.

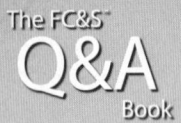
The insured has secured copies of the checks that are in dispute. They are made out to, endorsed, and cashed by the employee. I don't see anything in the policy that requires the original coding to remain in place to pay the claim. What recourse do we have?

Missouri subscriber

The insuring agreement states that payment is made for loss of or damage to money, securities, etc., resulting directly from theft committed by an employee, which is the situation here. The policy has no language requiring that coding not be altered; all that is required is that records be kept of all property covered, that a detailed sworn proof of loss be provided within 120 days, and that the named insured cooperate with the insurer in the investigation.

As to the denial based on lack of the original coding, you may want to consult an attorney to determine if there are requirements particular to your jurisdiction that apply over and above the policy language.

ERISA Coverage Needs

What forms or endorsements should be used to provide either excess ERISA or ERISA only coverage? In addition to listing the benefit plan on the policy declarations page, I have been informed that endorsement CR 25 31 should be attached to the CR 00 21. If this is the case, is the named insured or the plan name listed on the CR 25 31? If this approach is incorrect, please advise the proper method of providing excess ERISA or ERISA-only coverage. Thank you.

Michigan subscriber

CR 25 31 may be used to increase the limit of insurance that is required under ERISA for fidelity bonding of individuals handling money in a pension plan. As noted on the endorsement, the blanket excess limit entered in the schedule is in addition to the limit of insurance shown in the declarations. But it applies only to the insured entered in the schedule. So, for example, if the corporation carries a $100,000 employee dishonesty limit but needs a $300,000 limit to meet ERISA requirements, the pension plan would be entered in the schedule under "Insured" and the "Blanket Excess Limit of Insurance" would show $200,000.

However, we also found that the U.S. Department of Labor requires that the pension plan(s) be listed in the policy declarations as a named insured. So, endorsement CR 25 31 is not used to add the pension plan (as it must be a named insured) but, rather, to provide excess fidelity limits for specified joint insureds such as the pension plan.

Personal Cash Not Covered on Corporate Crime Policy

The president and owner of a company we insure withdrew cash from the company for personal use. He put it in a desk drawer, and later discovered it missing. The insured is a corporation covered on an ISO crime form that includes crime general provisions CR 10 00 06 95. Is there coverage for the loss of this money?

Ohio subscriber

Item 14 of the Crime General Conditions states that property covered is limited to property that *you* own or hold or for which *you* are legally liable (emphasis added). It further notes that *you* means the named insured.

Since this is a corporation, and the money was the owner's personal property when it was lost, there would be no coverage because it was not property owned by the named insured corporation at that point.

Theft of Money from Truck at Christmas Tree Stand Covered

A garden center that we insure operates a remote lot to sell Christmas trees. An employee is sent to the lot to drop off new trees and pick up the day's receipts, which he then takes back to the main location. Due to a heavy volume of business at the time, the designated messenger unloaded the trees and helped prepare them for sale. Simultaneously, another employee placed the day's receipts in a bag and put the bag in the driver's truck so it could be taken back to the main office.

The messenger employee finds the bag missing when he returns to the truck and presumes it has been stolen. He files a police report, which alleges theft by an outside party. Does the fact that a second employee and not the messenger put the money bag in the messenger's truck constitute giving the money into the "care and custody" of the messenger?

Wisconsin subscriber

We are answering this question by using the Outside the Premises wording on the ISO commercial crime policy, CR 00 20 07 02, which defines "messenger" to include the named insured, any relative, any partner or member, or any employee who has care and custody of money outside the premises. This form promises to cover money and other property while "outside the 'premises' in the care and custody of a 'messenger'" and resulting from "'theft,' disappearance or destruction." Care and custody is not defined on the policy.

It is our opinion that the fact that the money was transferred directly to the vehicle, bypassing the official messenger, does not negate the requirement that the money be in the care and custody of the messenger. However, we believe coverage still may depend upon whether the vehicle was locked or not. If it was not locked, it may not meet the requirement of "care and custody."

In *Home Indemnity Co. v. Desert Palace, Inc.*, 468 P.2d 19 (1970), the Supreme Court of Nevada cited the Georgia Court of Appeals case *Atlanta Tallow Co. v. Fireman's Fund. Ins. Co.*, 167 S.E.2d 361 (1969), in stating that "care and custody" did not mean "actual custody" but, rather, "protective custody." The requirement was satisfied by reasonable attempts to protect and secure the property. While acknowledging that some courts may require "personal custody," the Nevada court said it preferred the protective custody standard as long as the messenger took reasonable precautions in protecting the insured property from others. According to the court, "If appellant (Home Insurance) insists on personal, actual custody of the insured property at all times a messenger has custody, it can so word the contract of insurance." This case, and the others we found, used the standard of a locked vehicle and the messenger remaining engaged in work-related activities during the time of the loss as being reasonable care.

If the vehicle in question was locked, we believe that the money was in the care and custody of a messenger when stolen.

Deductible Question on Crime Settlement?

Is it proper to take two deductibles when part of the loss being paid by the current carrier fell within the coverage period of the prior carrier but was not discovered until after expiration of the discovery period?

Also, the CFO for the insured gave himself an unauthorized raise that was not approved by a superior. Would that be part "employee benefits earned in the normal course of employment" and therefore excluded or should that be considered part of the loss.

Maryland subscriber

Only one deductible typically is taken if the loss involves one occurrence or series of occurrences. In other words, if one employee or group of employees was taking money over a period of time, the loss typically would be considered one occurrence and only one deductible would be charged.

It is our opinion that salary, even though higher than officially authorized, is excluded if the form excludes benefits, including salary. The definition of "employee dishonesty" typically states that the employee benefits (including salary) earned in the normal course of employment are excluded. Since the salary is earned, even though higher than authorized, and earned in the normal course of employment, it does not appear as if this requirement was met.

Employee Dishonesty Spans Policies from Two Carriers

My insured had an employee dishonesty claim. The claim started in April of 2005 but was not discovered until February 21, 2006. The insurance was with ABC Mutual from September 9, 2003, to September 9, 2005. ABC Mutual pulled out of West Tennessee and we had to move the coverage, so XYZ Insurance covered the account from September 9, 2005-2006.

The total amount of the claim was around $98,000. XYZ's limit was $50,000, and it paid out $38,988.77, which was the amount taken during its policy period. ABC Mutual's limit was $15,000, but the adjuster has advised me the company is denying the claim based on the fact that we replaced coverage and that XYZ should pay more. XYZ says ABC Mutual should pick up the remaining portion.

Tennessee subscriber

We have reviewed the two employee dishonesty coverage provisions that you submitted, the one through ABC Mutual from 9/9/03-05 and the other, through XYZ Insurance, from 9/9/05-06. The loss, which was discovered in February of 2006, was perpetrated by a single employee over a period of time that bridged the two policy terms.

XYZ Insurance has paid nearly $39,000, which is the amount of loss that was sustained and discovered during its term. The remaining, unpaid claim amount of about $59,000 was sustained during the ABC Mutual term. The ABC Mutual policy is not liable because its one-year discovery period was terminated when the XYZ Insurance policy was instituted.

Looking to XYZ Insurance, its form under clause 2. h. states that it will pick up losses sustained during the policy period of "any prior insurance that you could have recovered under that insurance except that the time within which to discover loss or damage had expired . . ." This optional coverage provided through clause 2. h. does apply in this case because the loss would have been recovered under the ABC Mutual form except for the fact that it was replaced, and the discovery period terminated, by the XYZ Insurance policy.

Given that, we must then determine the amount that is available from XYZ Insurance on the prior sustained loss. The Optional Coverage for prior losses sustained but discovered during the XYZ Insurance term is included within, and not in addition to, its $50,000 limit. XYZ Insurance has paid $38,988.77.

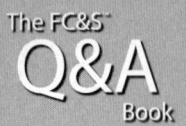

Therefore, there is an additional amount recoverable from XYZ Insurance of $11,011.23 on the loss sustained during the ABC Mutual term but discovered during the XYZ Insurance term.

Bond Forms Changes?

Have the Commercial Blanket and Blanket Position bonds been deleted and replaced with the employee theft and forgery forms? Under the Blanket Position bond coverage the limit of the bond applied separately per employee. Has this also changed?

Georgia subscriber

The commercial blanket and blanket position bonds have been replaced by corresponding forms through ISO. One such form is the Employee Theft and Forgery form (CR 00 29), as well as the Commercial Crime Coverage Forms (CR 00 20 and CR 00 21) and the Government Crime Forms (CR 00 24 and CR 00 25). The commercial crime and government crime forms are similar to the old Commercial Crime forms in that they offer various insuring agreements (employee theft, forgery, counterfeit, etc.)

These newer crime forms offer a number of endorsements that enable them to be converted to position or name schedules. For example, there are Employee Theft Name or Position endorsement (CR 04 08); Change Schedule endorsements (for example, CR 25 36) that permit adding coverage on a position or name schedule basis; schedule excess limits endorsements (CR 25 35 and CR 25 34), and Employee Theft – Per Loss Excess over Employee Theft – Per Employee. Some of these are dedicated to either the government or commercial crime forms; others may be available for use with either.

In addition, some carriers still may offer the commercial blanket and blanket position bonds, but you would have to ask your respective insurers if they are able to offer these.

The best way to approach this would be to indicate the type of coverage you are trying to arrange with your underwriter. Knowing that various endorsements do exist should enable you and your underwriter to negotiate the proper coverage.

Company President's Personal Funds Covered?

A specific insurance company crime form defines employee theft as follows: "means the unlawful taking of money, securities and other property to the deprivation of an Insured by an employee..."

122

One of our commercial accounts has its corporate bookkeeper take care of the personal account of the president and co-owner. The insurance company will not add the president as an insured. If the commercial named insured enters into a contractual agreement with the president to manage his personal account and assumes liability for losses caused by its employees, would the corporation's crime policy respond for a theft by the employee, stealing money from the president?

Pennsylvania subscriber

Without reviewing a complete copy of the policy, it is difficult to say whether the proposed contractual arrangement would provide coverage for the president's assets. The ISO commercial crime form, CR 00 20 03 00, states that the policy does NOT cover the following:

d. Indirect Loss

> Loss that is an indirect result of any act or "occurrence" covered by this insurance including, but not limited to, loss resulting from:

(1) Your inability to realize income that you would have realized had there been no loss of or damage to "money", "securities", or "other property".

(2) Payment of damages of any type for which you are legally liable. But, we will pay compensatory damages arising directly from a loss covered under this insurance.

(3) Payment of costs, fees or other expenses you incur in establishing either the existence or the amount of loss under this insurance.

Item d.(2) precludes payment for damages for which the named insured is legally liable. If such a clause is included in the policy covering this risk, there would be an argument against coverage.

However, the overriding problem we see is that the carrier already has indicated it does not want to cover this exposure by declining to add the president as an insured. Absent an applicable exclusion for contractual liability coverage on the form, you still might run into a problem if the carrier believed the arrangement constituted a material misrepresentation of what was being insured. Therefore, we would run a potential contractual solution to the dilemma past the underwriter before setting it up.

If the carrier is willing to accept the exposure but just does not want to add the president as an insured, there might be endorsements that could cover the exposure even without a contractual assumption of liability. In the commercial crime program, there are endorsements to include coverage for client's property, as well as for the property of others. Such an endorsement might take care of this situation.

Recovery Divided under What Basis?

We have a situation in which an employee embezzled some money. The insurer has not paid anything; a formal claim has not even been submitted by the insured. The employee is bonded at $20,000. The initial loss appears to be in excess of $300,000. Some recovery has been made and more, I believe, is expected.

Under the Commercial Crime Coverage Form, Conditions, Recoveries: conditions of recoveries are defined "after settlement" has been made.

How would recoveries be distributed prior to settlement by the insurer?

South Carolina subscriber

The recovery section of the commercial crime form outlines the division of funds recovered through subrogation. An insurer cannot subrogate until it has paid a loss, and then it can subrogate only to the extent of its payment. So, if the insurer has not paid out anything, it is not entitled to subrogation.

Therefore, if, as you say, the total loss is $300,000, but, upon discovery, the embezzler has returned say, $100,000, the amount of loss at that point would be $200,000. If the insurer does eventually pay its $20,000 limit, it would be subrogated to the insured's rights to the tune of $20,000. In this example, since the $200,000 loss ($300,000-$100,000 recovered before claim made) exceeds the limit of coverage ($20,000) the insured would be reimbursed the $20,000 less the insurer's cost to recover that amount under item (1) a. of the policy form.

Volunteers Covered for Crime Exposures?

I have a client with no employees, just a volunteer board of directors.

The question of crime and money and securities came up. I don't think these exposures would be covered under commercial crime because of the definition of employee in the crime policy. Am I right?

Wisconsin subscriber

You don't specify what form, but if it's a current ISO form, you are correct. Employees on the current ISO form(s) CR 00 22 03 00 and CR 00 23 03 00 are natural persons who are compensated for their work, etc.

If it is one of those forms, you could use CR 25 09 03 00 or CR 25 10 03 00 to add volunteer workers, depending on whether the volunteers are fund solicitors.

WORKERS COMPENSATION

Workers Compensation and Parking Lot Injury

We have an insured with an employee who was off duty and leaving work. The employee was in the parking lot on her way to the car when she fell on the ice. The employee broke her wrist. Should workers compensation pay this?

Arkansas subscriber

It is our opinion that this injury, which occurred in the employer's parking lot after the employee had left work for the day, is not compensable under Arkansas statute.

The 1993 Arkansas workers compensation amendments deleted the premises exception to the going and coming rule. Therefore, even though the employee was on the employer's premises at the time of injury, she does not appear to have been performing employment services and, therefore, her injury would not be compensable.

The court, in *Hightower v. Newark Public School System*, 943 S.W.2d 608 (1997) reasoned that Ark. Code Ann. § 11-9-102(4)(B)(iii) excludes from being compensable injuries that occur "at a time when employment services were not being performed." According to the *Hightower* court, this provision eliminates the premises exception to the going-and-coming rule since, under a strict construction of Arkansas Code, merely walking to and from one's car, even on the employer's premises, does not qualify as performing "employment services." (emphasis added).

Keep in mind, however, that if the employee was acting at the direction of her employer, an exception for compensability might be inferred. For example, in *Caffey v. Sanyo Mfg. Corp.*, 154 S.W.3d 274 (2004), the Arkansas appeals court held that the employer was performing employment services after entering the parking lot. In this case, although the employee was not yet being paid, she was required to exhibit her identification before entry into the parking lot, and, after parking her vehicle, she was required by her employer to walk to a guard shack and again display her identification, and then claimant was required to clock in. Although all of these were requirements of her employer, the claimant was not paid until she was at her work station. However, the court ruled that payment for these services was not determinative of "employment services."

You did not indicate any such circumstances, however, so we do not believe that simply falling in the parking lot after ending the work day is compensable in Arkansas.

⊛ Employers Liability Situations Outlined

What are the most common EL claim scenarios? How would you define this coverage in layman's terms?

Alabama subscriber

Employers liability insurance applies to injuries that arise out of employment situations but which fall outside the scope of the applicable state's workers compensation statutes. Generally, such injuries fall within one of several classes:

1) the insured's liability for damages claimed against a third party by one of the insured's employees (these are called "third-party-over" actions);

2) damages assessed for care and loss of services, such as loss of consortium; and

3) consequential bodily injury to a spouse, child, parent, brother, or sister of the injured employee.

Third-party over actions may occur as a result of contractual hold harmless agreements in which employers assume the liability of parties for whom they are working. If an employee is injured on this job, he may be eligible for workers compensation benefits, but he also may sue the other party (for example, the owner of the project) for negligence. If the owner of the project is held harmless by the injured employee's employer, the suit may be turned over to the employer, resulting in a third-party over action and potential employers liability coverage or defense.

In addition, the employers liability section covers damages assessed "because of bodily injury to your employee that arises out of and in the course of employment, claimed against you (the insured) in a capacity other than as employer." These are called dual capacity actions, situations in which an employee is injured as a result of employment but the injury is caused by an action not resulting solely from the insured's status as the employer. A typical example that frequently is given in dual capacity cases is that of an employee whose employer manufactures tires. An employee is changing a tire during work, using an employer-manufactured tire, and the tire blows, injuring the worker. Although the injury may be related to work, the tire is a product of the manufacturer-employer. The employer may be liable as the manufacturer in such a situation and thus have a dual capacity.

These types of damages correspond well with certain exclusions found on the commercial general liability (CGL) coverage forms. The CGL forms specifically exclude damages to be paid due to any obligation of the insured under a workers compensation law; the forms exclude coverage for bodily injury to

GL EXCLS, Injury to employee

an employee of the insured (or to an employee's spouse, child, parent, etc. for consequential bodily injury) that arises out of and in the course of employment by the insured; and the exclusions apply whether the insured may be liable either as an employer or in any other capacity (dual capacity), and they apply to any obligation to share damages with or repay someone else who must pay damages (third-party-over actions).

There are a number of discussions in *FC&S* on this subject. If you have the online version, enter employers liability in the phrase search box, and several discussions will be highlighted.

Workers Compensation Coverage and Shooting Deaths

We have an insured who was found shot to death at his place of employment along with one of his employees. We had the carrier open up two Massachusetts workers comp claims on the premise of presumption of workers compensation claims when they were found dead at the workplace.

It turns out they apprehended the murderer, and the incident has to do with his desire to be with the insured's wife. I have asked the carrier to close the insured's claim based on the fact that it was not causally related to work.

However, I believe that the employee's claim would be covered as he was in harm's way due to his employment. I do not believe this applies to the insured.

Massachusetts subscriber

You did not state whether this insured was a corporation, sole proprietorship, or partnership. However, under Massachusetts law, corporate officers are subject to the workers compensation law unless they have officially opted out. Sole proprietors and partners may elect coverage but are not required to do so.

Given that, we are assuming that the "insured" you mentioned was covered by the workers compensation law of Massachusetts and was insured for that exposure.

We could not find case law specific to Massachusetts but did find two cases (one from Minnesota and one from Texas) that, while not completely on point, offer some potential guidance.

The Minnesota case, *Fernandez v. Ramsey County*, dealt with sexual assault and battery. The court stated that the question of whether the injury arose out of and in the course of employment turned on the facts of the case. If the "alleged intent to injure is for personal reasons or directed against employee

as an employee" would determine whether workers compensation was the sole remedy or not. In this case, the court ruled that there were enough questions surrounding the injury to preclude summary judgment.

The Texas case, *Sanders v. Texas Employers Insurance Association*, dealt with a personal assault upon an individual after he was dismissed as an employee. The court stated that the termination of employee status precluded workers compensation coverage.

Neither of these cases, as stated previously, is from Massachusetts and neither exactly mimics the facts of your case. However, we recommend you consider the following in making your case to have the insured's claim closed:

1. Has the case been adjudicated and murder for personal reasons been judicially established? If the murder case is closed through adjudication there seems less need to retain a workers compensation reserve for the insured.

2. Did the murderer ever work at the insured's location? If so, this could move the claim closer to workers compensation.

3. Has it been proven that the murderer went to the location with the sole purpose of murdering the insured because of a love triangle? Or, for example, did the murderer go there to burglarize or vandalize the place, the insured tried to stop the burglary/vandalism, and then was shot? This type of situation could move it closer to a workers compensation situation.

Our concern is that, if the case has not been adjudicated and the facts legally memorialized, there is a chance that an employment-related nexus could be established.

Based on this, we wonder if the carrier would reduce the reserve but keep the claim open for informational purposes only. It seems unlikely from the details you presented that this is a work-related situation, but there is an outside chance if it has not yet been adjudicated. Because of that we believe it would be wise to keep the claim open "for the record" but reduce the reserve.

Spouse Covered for Workers Compensation?

The owner of a business we insure has elected to cover himself under workers compensation. The insured's spouse works in the office and has reported her income for years. Is she covered under workers compensation for work-related injuries if she hasn't signed an election-to-cover form? Although she is the spouse she is not an owner of the company.

Nebraska subscriber

Your question depends upon the employee status of the wife. All Nebraska employers (except certain exempt classifications) are covered by the workers compensation law if they have at least one employee. Even if the insured employer is exempt, she would be covered if she is an employee and if a workers compensation policy is in place.

Exempt employers, such as certain agricultural operations and railroads, are addressed by the Nebraska workers compensation statute §48-101, et al. As noted in section 48-106, even those employers that are exempt fall within the law if they elect to purchase a workers compensation insurance policy:

> "(6) An employer who is exempt from the act under subsection (2) of this section may elect to bring the employees of such employer under the act. Such election is made by the employer obtaining a policy of workers' compensation insurance covering such employees. Such policy shall be obtained from a corporation, association, or organization authorized and licensed to transact the business of workers' compensation insurance in this state. If such an exempt employer procures a policy of workers' compensation insurance which is in full force and effect at the time of an accident to an employee of such employer, such procurement is conclusive proof of the employer's and employee's election to be bound by the act. . ."

So, if the business is exempt from the law, the spouse is covered if there is a workers compensation policy in place and if she is an employee. The law requires that employees be covered if the employer is not exempt.

P&I Policy and Lakeside Employer

We write the workers compensation, including the USL&H endorsement, for a policyholder who does work on the shore of Lake Superior. The company also does work from a barge off shore. Our policyholder provides coverage for the barge employees through a Protection & Indemnity (P&I) policy. As an ocean marine coverage, how does this provide workers compensation benefits to employees?

Michigan subscriber

The P&I coverage could be used to provide liability coverage for the insured for injury to employees, who, if considered to be seamen, could be covered by the Jones Act.

The USL&H endorsement extends the Part 1 of the workers compensation policy to apply to the Longshore and Harbor Workers Compensation Act as

well as the applicable state workers compensation law. As you stated, this endorsement is attached to the workers compensation policy.

There is a Maritime Coverage Endorsement, which also can be attached to the workers comp policy. However, the Maritime Coverage Endorsement affects the Part Two, Employers Liability, coverage. The endorsement deletes exclusion 10 of the employers liability section, which states that the unendorsed Employers Liability coverage does not apply to "bodily injury to a master or member of the crew of any vessel." By attaching the Maritime Coverage Endorsement, the exclusion is deleted and Employers Liability coverage applies to that category of employee.

However, the Maritime Coverage Endorsement also adds two exclusions, one of which states that bodily injury covered by a P&I (or similar) policy is not covered by the endorsement. So, if the insured carried both, the P&I policy typically would be used to address applicable employee injuries. Keep in mind that an employee would have to be considered a "master or member of the crew" in order for these coverages to be applicable.

P&I coverage is used to provide liability coverage for bodily injury to members of the crew and to third parties, as well as property damage coverage. It would respond to a suit by an employee for injury aboard a vessel. In addition, an employee may be able to sue the vessel, itself, for liability for bodily injury. This is called an in rem action. P&I policies would be one way to cover that potential exposure.

There are several *FC&S Online* articles that provide more information on this topic. These may assist you further to properly insure these exposures.

Hockey Officials Employees or Independent Contractors?

I am gathering information about whether a college-level hockey association should or could obtain workers compensation for the on-ice officials. Part of the issue is that the officials do this as a part-time job. At the current time there is no insurance coverage, and if they were seriously injured they would perhaps lose their income from both hockey and their full-time jobs if they were unable to work.

So to be clear, an official is seriously injured while working for the hockey organization and is not able to perform his full time job. Would he be able to receive compensation from his full-time employer if that employer had workers compensation? The states involved are Massachusetts, New Hampshire, and Rhode Island.

Massachusetts subscriber

All three states you mention—Massachusetts, New Hampshire, and Rhode Island—consider that the average weekly wage used for computing compensation for employees in the concurrent service of more than one employer is based on total earnings from the several employers. This is limited by state maximum payment levels. (See M.G.L.A. 152 section 1; N.H. Rev. Stat. section 281-A:15; and RI St section 28-33-20.)

You stated that the league considers the ice officials independent contractors. If the ice officials are independent contractors, they would not be eligible for workers compensation coverage, which is available only to employees. The question of whether individuals are employees or independent contractors is a legal one but typically is based on the issue of control—who controls the work situation and the relationship between the one exercising control and the injured party.

For income tax purposes, the IRS has a checklist to determine the status of the worker:

A.   Who delivers instructions and who complies with them;

B.   How training is done;

C.   Where direction and control come from;

D.   Who does the hiring, supervising, and paying;

E.   Who sets the hours of work;

F.   Who has the right to discharge a worker and terminate the work;

G.   Who furnishes the tools and materials to do the work; and

H.   Who supplies the investment or capital to do the work?

As you can see, the payment process is just one of the items to be considered. If the workers qualify for workers compensation coverage, they give up the right to other forms of satisfaction in the event of injury.

We cannot determine whether the ice officials you mention are employees or independent contractors. But a discussion in *FC&S Online*, "Compensation Liability of Principals and Contractors," may be helpful to you in further analyzing their status.

Back-dated WC Policy Considered to be Insurance?

We are handling a situation in which an employee was injured, but workers compensation coverage was not in place at the time of injury because of an error on the part of the insurance agent.

The employee sued her employer for negligence and for compensatory damages. The employer sued the agent for E&O.

Eighteen months later the agent convinced an affiliated insurer to issue a workers compensation policy with no premium payment as an accommodation. The underwriter said no standards were used because the issuance was done at corporate counsel's request.

The insurer and agent are separate corporations within the same holding company system.

Does this constitute "insurance" under the "known loss" doctrine? Does it defeat the employee's claim based on a lack of "insurance" being in place?

Michigan subscriber

The workers compensation policy does not reference known losses, so, if the policy was back-dated to include the date of loss, coverage should be available for it. The known loss doctrine, as discussed in the *FC&S Online* article on The Montrose Endorsement, pertains to situations in which the insured knew of a loss—or an incident that likely would result in a loss—but did not advise the underwriter of the situation before a policy was written. However, this is not the case here. From what you explained, the underwriter was fully aware that she would be picking up the workers compensation loss when she issued a back-dated policy.

The question of whether the issuance of the policy would defeat the injured employee's negligence claim is a legal issue, and we cannot specifically address legal issues. Many issues could enter into this, such as whether the claimant suffered because of the lack of coverage over and above the original injury, whether the state regulatory agency was involved, whether fines already had been assessed, etc.